SETTING THE RECORD STRAIGHT

Responses to Misconceptions About Public Education in the United States

GERALD W. BRACEY

ASCD

Association for Supervision and Curriculum Development

Alexandria, Virginia

ASCD

Association for Supervision and Curriculum Development
1250 N. Pitt Street • Alexandria, Virginia 22314-1453
Telephone: 1-800-933-2723 or 703-549-9110 • Fax: 703-299-8631

Gene R. Carter, *Executive Director*
Michelle Terry, *Assistant Executive Director, Program Development*
Ronald S. Brandt, *Assistant Executive Director*
Nancy Modrak, *Manager, Publications*
John O'Neil, *Acquisitions Editor*
Julie Houtz, *Managing Editor of Books*
Kathleen Larson Florio, *Copy Editor*
Gary Bloom, *Manager, Design and Production Services*
Karen Monaco, *Designer*
Tracey A. Smith, *Production Coordinator*
Dina Murray, *Production Assistant*
Barton, Matheson, Willse, & Worthington, *Typesetter*
Sarah A. Smith, *Indexer*

ASCD publications present a variety of viewpoints. The views expressed or implied
in this book should not be interpreted as official positions of the Association.

Printed in the United States of America.

February 1997 member book (p). ASCD Premium, Comprehensive, and Regular
members periodically receive ASCD books as part of their membership benefits.
No. FY97-5.

ASCD Stock No.: 197020   ASCD member price: $16.95   nonmember price: $20.95

Library of Congress Cataloging-in-Publication Data
Bracey, Gerald W.
   Setting the record straight : responses to misconceptions about public educa-
tion in the United States / Gerald W. Bracey.
      p. cm.
   Includes bibliographical references and index.
   ISBN 0-87120-279-4 (pbk.)
   1. Public schools—United States.   2. Academic achievement—United States.
3. Education—United States—Finance.   I. Title.
LA217.2.B73   1996
371.01'0973—dc21   96-51260
                                                                         CIP

00 99 98 97   5 4 3 2 1

S E T T I N G
T H E
R E C O R D
S T R A I G H T

Responses to Misconceptions
About Public Education in the United States

Introduction - - - - - - - - - - - - - - - 1
1. Hey, Big Spender - - - - - - - - - - - 13
2. Throwing Money at the Schools - - - 20
3. Rising Costs, Flat Scores - - - - - - - 28
4. "Plummeting" SAT Scores - - - - - - 43
5. The Shrinking SAT Elite - - - - - - - 58
6. Knowledge Nostalgia - - - - - - - - - 66
7. International Comparisons - - - - - - 75
8. The Dropout Rate - - - - - - - - - - 112
9. Private Versus Public Schools - - - 119
10. Choice and Charter Schools - - - - 133
11. The Global Marketplace - - - - - - 151
12. Preparing Students for Work - - - 162
13. The Shortage of Scientists - - - - - 167
14. The Administrative Blob - - - - - - 171
15. Teacher Accountability - - - - - - - 175
16. Dumb Teachers - - - - - - - - - - - 180
17. "Feel Good" Education - - - - - - - 184
18. Special Education Costs - - - - - - 191
Epilogue - - - - - - - - - - - - - - - - - 194
List of Figures - - - - - - - - - - - - - - 198
Appendix A: More Recent Figures
      on Spending - - - - - - - - - - - - 201
Index - - - - - - - - - - - - - - - - - - - 203
About the Author - - - - - - - - - - - - 215

Introduction

A number of publications—the six existing "Bracey Reports on the Condition of Public Education" that have appeared in *Phi Delta Kappan* each October beginning in 1991; David Berliner and Bruce Biddle's *The Manufactured Crisis;* Joe Schneider and Paul Houston's *Exploding the Myths;* the "Sandia Report," which appeared in the May/June 1993 issue of the *Journal of Educational Research;* and various articles by Berliner, Iris Rotberg, Harold Howe, Harold Hodgkinson, and Richard Jaeger— have begotten new awareness in the educational community that U.S. schools are doing much better than people think they are (while pointing to some areas where they are actually doing worse). In addition, the Center for Educational Development and Research at Phi Delta Kappa has recently issued a compendium of such articles, called *Straight Talk About America's Schools: Dispelling the Myths.* Signs indicate that even the media are taking note: articles about the work of the above-listed "revisionists" have appeared in *Newsweek* (Robert Samuelson, December 4, 1995), the *New York Times* (Peter Applebome, December 14, 1995), the *Washington Post* (Gerald Bracey, December 22, 1995), and *Better Homes and Gardens* (Nick Gallo, March 1996).

A need remains, however, to provide teachers, administrators, and school board members with a tool that is targeted toward specific issues, myths, and slanders that are often aimed at the schools. In January and February of 1996, for example, misleading full-page ads appeared in the *New York Times* painting a bad and distorted picture of public schools in the United States. The ad was sponsored by the National Alliance of Business, the Business Roundtable, the National Governors Association, the American Federation of Teachers, and the U.S. Department of Education. In response, I wrote a rebuttal, "With Friends Like These," but no one deigned to publish it.

Those who continue to criticize the schools continue to utter statements that are simply untrue. In his July 11, 1996, speech on education, presidential candidate Robert Dole declared that test scores are falling (false), dropout rates are rising (false), and illiteracy is increasing (false). According to reports on National Public Radio, the speech was written by two former secretaries of education, William Bennett and Lamar Alexander, who "sat nearby, smiling as the speech was delivered." Louis V. Gerstner, CEO of IBM, keeps running around the country saying the system is broken and declaring that if schools don't shape up, the U.S. economy, the most competitive in the world and the envy of every nation, will soon be a third world affair. The Heritage Foundation's *The Candidate's Handbook, 1996* provided material for conservatives seeking to get elected. In the section on education, Denis Doyle penned a number of statements that are not true and, in passing, dismissed *The Manufactured Crisis* and called me "Chicken Little in Reverse." Former Assistant Secretary of Education Chester E. Finn Jr. now writes his rhetoric out of the conservative Hudson Institute and has declared that education reform "is a cultural, intellectual, and ideological war." Ideologues, it should be noted, are not generally interested in facts that refute their position, and Finn has shown no interest in moderating his stance on the basis of real data.

In addition, a coalition of businesspeople and governors seems bent on privatizing our schools. These actors see all human interaction in terms of commercial transactions. They are not interested in the fact that their approach is, at root, totalitarian. They do not understand the communal needs of a democracy and how public schools alone can fulfill this need in society. This problem is discussed at length in Chapter 10.

At the risk of seeming to overdo the issue, I wish to emphasize that educators must open their eyes to the intensity of the anti-school efforts. Those who oppose public schooling generally state their goals openly, so we cannot call their efforts a *conspiracy,* but we should recognize the highly organized dissemination plans they use to advance their views.

In August 1996, a study appeared purporting to show that the school choice program in Milwaukee, Wisconsin, was working well, although five years of evaluations had failed to find positive outcomes. The cover of the report states that it was prepared for a meeting of the American Political Science Association. But the study first appeared not at this professional meeting, nor in a professional journal, but as a wire-service story from the Associated Press—two weeks before the APSA meeting was to take place. An article by the same authors just happened to appear the very same day as an op-ed piece in the *Wall Street Journal*. Shall we assume this magnificent timing was an accident? I think not. This same day also just happened to be the day that presidential candidate Bob Dole delivered his education speech to the Republic National Convention, a speech that, in part, called for school choice.

William Bennett and Lamar Alexander quickly hyped the study on television and noted pedagogue Rush Limbaugh dispersed it over the airwaves. The conservative quarterly *The Public Interest* managed to have the authors of the study write an essay about their work in the fall 1996 issue. Since *The Public Interest* has a lead time of three months and the fall issue is shipped in mid-September, the editors must have had the story in hand well before any of the other media published it.

Obviously, the intent of the authors of the study was to foreclose discussion of the results until their own views had been widely spread through the nation. Such dissemination, of course, seriously compromises any later attempts to rebut the study. The deed has been done. (The study, incidentally, did *not* show that the Milwaukee choice program was good for students).

This book provides a defense against those who innocently attack schools with always abundant misinformation, and those, like Doyle and Finn (and others), who disingenuously attack schools with disinformation.

The Plan of This Book

After speeches I am often asked questions that take the form of "What do you say when someone says X?" "X" designates some common criticism of the schools.

This book offers 18 such common criticisms. Each chapter addresses one. A discussion of the criticism and its sources is followed by a brief suggested reply. These brief replies contain little or no data, just the proper response. But, of course, in order not to be successfully challenged, you must have the data at hand. Thus, after the brief replies, I lay out all of the data pertinent to the issue. I have tried to keep these elaborations as brief as possible without sacrificing their comprehensiveness. In some cases, however, such as the comparisons between American schools and those of other nations, the discussion is necessarily long. The criticism of schools has gone on so long that a simple statistic is not likely to convince a critic. *You need to know your stuff.* There is no substitute for familiarity with the data and the issue.

Two other publications present similar data, but each has its shortcomings. The recent pamphlet "The Good—and the Not So Good—News About American Schools" is a good start at rethinking what the data say, but it is no more than that (Jennings 1996). Its 25 pages contain a number of useful facts; but these facts are not organized with the purpose of refuting specific contentions, and the pamphlet does not address many of the myths dealt with in this book. *The Manufactured Crisis* (Berliner and Biddle 1995), on the other hand, contains almost too much data for the purposes at hand. It is a thorough and scholarly work—scholarly in the sense of comprehensiveness, I hasten to add, not in the sense of impenetrable prose. It is a highly readable book and an excellent reference document to back up this one.

After the presentation of the data, brief replies "in sum" reiterate the replies presented earlier in the chapter, but can now be read with the just-presented data in mind.

At the end of each chapter is a list of references for all of the works mentioned in the text. Most readers likely will have neither the time nor the need to delve so deeply into the issues, but being able to cite a reference is, in itself, a means of establishing credibility. And there may be some occasions, such as when the district or the state debates choice or charter schools, when it will be important to know what the disinterested writers have had to say on the topic.

The Epilogue provides some perspective on what has happened over the previous pages. What does the book, in general, say and not say about the condition of schools and the status of reform efforts? The book does not say, for instance, that things are OK and that therefore the reform efforts can be called to a halt. Quite the contrary. But it does urge that reform efforts move forward without the all-too-common "The Beatings Will Continue Until Morale Improves" mentality that has afflicted so many reform undertakings.

This book makes no claim to being comprehensive, although it does deal with a goodly number of vexing issues. But it is silent on many other contentions about schools: bilingualism does (does not) work; discipline is missing in the schools; teachers unions are the principal obstacle to reform; and so forth. The book does not address such issues simply because no good data are available to resolve the debate. The myths that are treated on these pages are those for which the body of data is sufficient either to compel a conclusion or to lean heavily in one direction.

Some of these other issues *should* be investigated and would make good research topics. For instance, surveys conducted by the Public Agenda organization indicate a large concern with discipline. Is discipline a problem? Is it a widespread problem? Is it more of a problem now than it was 25 years ago, or are teachers simply more comfortable with letting kids be kids and not imposing arbitrary and restrictive limits on young people? Good questions all, but not the kind that can today be answered with data; hence, not the kind to be dealt with in this book.

That being said, we make something of an exception for a brief excursion into the realm of standards. We do this only because the issues surrounding standards appear to be those that will dominate conversations about education reform in the near future. We cannot determine the impact of standards yet, but we can, hopefully, shed some light on what to look for.

The issues surrounding standards have taken on a new sense of importance since the July 1996 meeting of the National Governors Association (NGA). At their meeting, the governors formally approved the establishment of some kind of "entity" (at the moment it has no other name) to help states develop standards. The entity will assist states and businesses to receive "technical assistance in the areas of standards, assessments, accountability, and the use of technology in schools" (Lawton 1996). All four areas figured large in the conversations of an earlier NGA meeting.

In October 1996, the entity was given the name "Achieve" and its stated purpose is to be a national clearinghouse in the areas named above. Specifically, according to an October 16, 1996 press release, "Achieve" will do the following:

> Provide national leadership on the issues of high academic standards, assessments, accountability, and effective use of technology to achieve high standards;
> Prepare and make publicly available an annual report that tracks progress made towards achieving the commitments made at the 1996 Education Summit;
> Establish and manage an electronic clearinghouse of information on academic standards, assessment tools, and accountability systems used by various states and countries;
> Provide a benchmarking program to compare standards and assessment tools among states and internally; and
> Provide technical assistance to states seeking to establish and meet higher academic standards.

"Achieve" has received some $5 million in pledges from some of industry's heavy hitters—IBM, AT&T, and Proctor and Gamble, to name a few. Frankly, $5 million—even $5 million annually—won't contribute significantly to the accomplishment of the goals outlined above.

The interest in and concern for standards began at the national level shortly after World War II, when some commentators linked schools to the space and weapons races with the Soviet Union. Schools had always come in for their share of criticism, but now it took a new tack. Prior to World War II, there was nothing in the critiques to suggest that schools had ever educated students any better than they currently did. After World War II, one began to see indications that critics thought there had once been a finer era. In the most influential book of the day, for example, historian Arthur Bestor (1953) signaled the concern with this title: *Educational Wastelands: The Retreat From Learning in Public Schools.* No one had suggested retreat before.

Typical of the Cold War rhetoric of the day were Admiral Hyman Rickover's speeches in which he repeatedly reminded the United States of the danger: "Let us never forget that there can be no second place in a contest with Russia and that there will be no second chance if we lose" (Rickover 1959, p. 45). Rickover saw the schools as the principal engine driving the space and weapons races—an engine with little horsepower.

When into this anxious atmosphere the Russians launched *Sputnik,* the first man-made satellite, it was proof to the critics that schools had decayed from the standards to which they had once been held. The March 24, 1958, issue of *Life* magazine contained a feature called "Crisis in Education," which compared the U.S. and Soviet school systems by observing the life of two teenagers, one in a Moscow school, one in Chicago. The Moscow lad is clearly held to high standards and is shown conducting complicated experiments in physics and chemistry. The American student is depicted as having an academically easy time of it. One picture shows him laughing as he departs from a blackboard. The text reads: "Stephen amused his classmates with wisecracks about his ineptitude in mathematics."

Life gave two full pages of small print to novelist Sloan Wilson's description of the emergency:

> The facts of the school crisis are all out in plain sight and pretty dreadful to look at. First of all it has been shown that a surprisingly small percentage of high school students is studying what used to be considered basic subjects. . . . People are complaining that the diploma has been devaluated to the point of meaninglessness. . . . It is hard to deny that America's schools, which were supposed to reflect one of history's noblest dreams and to cultivate the nation's youthful minds, have degenerated into a system for coddling and entertaining the mediocre (Wilson 1958, pp. 36–37).

Wilson had discovered a "rising tide of mediocrity" 25 years before it would be noticed in *A Nation At Risk*.[1]

In the history of American educational reform, each new set of reformers has usually ignored everything that happened earlier. So it was with Willard Wirtz and Archie Lapointe, who took their starting place as the 1970s, but nevertheless captured well the thinking about U.S. education in their 1982 publication:

> By the early 1970s, the national sense developed that educational quality was deteriorating rapidly and dangerously. It is not entirely clear how far this went, how general it was, or what measure of fault was the schools'. But the judgment was made clearly and firmly. The reaction to this alarm took a dramatically new form. For reasons rooted in other developments, many people had lost confidence in the government and in the professions. The strongly sensed deterioration in education seemed confirmation of the failures of both of these services. So it was decided not to rely this time on either of these agencies. The decision, instead, in one state and community after another, was to move in directly on the schools, not with funds, but with *"standards"* (p. 2).

Given the mentality described by Wirtz and Lapointe, it is not surprising that the appearance in 1983 of *A Nation at Risk* caused such a stir. *Risk* called for increasing standards in a variety of areas: more and tougher courses, longer school years, and so forth. It did not spell out what, precisely, students should learn except to recommend more study of computers. *Risk* launched a flurry of reforms cast in terms of "more": more math, more science, and so forth. In 1989 the governors met with then-President George Bush at the first "Education Summit" and adopted six National Education Goals, some of which look very much like setting standards: "In the year 2000 U.S. students will be first in the world in science and mathematics." This is a normative statement; we will judge the standard of our stu-

---

[1] A more detailed examination of this period and, indeed, of a century of educational criticism and reform can be found in Bracey 1995.

dents' achievement in relation to performances in other nations. Other standard-development procedures have tried to specify what students should learn without reference to any external group.

After the summit, a group called the National Education Goals Panel was established to decide how we might reach our goals and how we might assess our children to see if, indeed, we had reached them. The National Goals were given a programmatic name, "Goals 2000." When Clinton defeated Bush in 1992, the name was changed to "America 2000: Educate America Act," but the six goals were left intact, and two were added later. This was not a surprise, even given the political differences between Bush and Clinton: Clinton had been governor of Arkansas and chair of the NGA at the time of the summit.

During this same interval, however, some groups started reacting negatively to another standards-oriented movement, outcomes-based education (OBE). Whereas OBE advocates claimed that they were establishing outcomes that would result in all students learning to high standards, OBE opponents claimed just the opposite—that the only way to teach all kids the same things was not to teach any of them very much. (See Chapter 17 for more about this anti-OBE argument.)

At the same time, some OBE programs were "caught" in the act of measuring affective as well as cognitive outcomes. This led to accusations that the schools were attempting to control the minds and behavior of children, were interfering in matters that should be left to the family, and were setting the stage for a national curriculum and a federal takeover of education. In some quarters the specter of a federal takeover of schools, bad enough in itself, was seen as only a prelude to the surrender of sovereignty by the federal government to the United Nations. For some groups, George Bush's declaration of a "New World Order" had taken on extremely sinister connotations.

The validity of the pro- and con-OBE arguments is not at issue here. The controversies, however, had the impact of tainting the national standards movement. Those who still favored national standards attempted to make a distinction between "national" standards that would be developed by professionals and used voluntarily by states and localities, and "federal" standards that would issue from the federal government. To no avail.

When the Second Education Summit took place in March 1996, the governors, most of whom had not been elected at the time of the first summit, forcefully moved to transfer the standards momentum from the White House to the state house. It is not yet clear what will happen at the state level, but any number of governors— Michigan's John Engler, Wisconsin's Tommy Thompson, Pennsylvania's Tom Ridge, Virginia's George Allen, Colorado's Roy Romer— are forcefully pushing the standards movement at the state level.

Will standards improve learning? One can say only "possibly" and "it depends." A survey by the American Federation of Teachers in August 1996 concluded that only 15 states deserved a "passing grade" in establishing standards. Critics of the survey immediately noted that the grades depended on how specific the standards were, not how challenging they were. No data have been collected yet, one way or another.

The standards that have been developed to date by professional organizations such as the National Council of Teachers of Mathematics, the National Council of Teachers of English, the National Science Teachers Association, and the National Council for the Social Studies differ wildly in their attention to specificity versus challenge. It is not clear how the states will deal with this variability.

Standards can improve learning if they give teachers clear ideas about what the best minds in the curriculum areas think it is important to teach, if they give teachers ways of incorporating the standards into daily classroom practice, if they increase the range of ideas that teachers can draw on, and if the teachers themselves "buy into" the standards as valid. This is a tall order.

Standards might have a negative outcome in terms of increasing the gaps in achievement between rich and poor districts. Districts with a modicum of affluence are likely to form committees to review the standards from the professional groups and report back to the superintendent, the school board, or the teaching faculty regarding which aspects of the standards the committee thinks are worthwhile for the district to incorporate into its curriculum. Similarly, if standards are imposed by state mandate, committees will assess how best to implement them.

On the other hand, in districts where schools are being closed because they are fire hazards, where the plumbing doesn't work, where there are no laboratories, where textbooks are obsolete or nonexistent, where homework cannot be assigned because of the lack of textbooks, where shelves are collapsing because termites have eaten them, or where the athletic field is squishy from the septic tank underneath—these schools have more basic, urgent concerns.

When it comes to determining if the standards have been met or have improved learning, competing forces will pull states in opposite directions. States compete for business and industries. It will be important for governors to show CEOs—as well as state boards and local politicians—that students in the state are meeting the standards. This mitigates against high standards. Conversely, some states may wish to impress visiting committees and local politicians with the toughness of their standards, not the attainment rate.

It should be an interesting time.

Earlier I noted that standards can be absolute, defined in terms of what students should know, or normative, defined in relation to the performance of other groups. In fact, standards are much more complicated than most conversations about them make it sound. One hears standards this, standards that as if there were a single definition of "standard" and everyone was clear on what it meant. In fact, there are a variety of ways of defining standards. In my 1995 book *Final Exam: A Study of the Perpetual Scrutiny of American Education*, I devote a whole section to the evolution of standards, including eight pages on how standards can be defined, standards versus standardization, and so forth. For the purposes of this book, however, I think the issues surrounding standards can be summarized by the following quote:

> The lack of standards is education's dirty little secret. . . . Many countries are educating everybody to higher levels than we are. One of the main differences between us and them is standards: they have them and we don't (Spillane 1993).

This statement by Fairfax County (Virginia) Schools superintendent Robert Spillane captures a lot of the feeling about standards.

Spillane is factually wrong both in his assertion about the accomplishments of other nations and in terms of the universality of standards in these other nations. This book will show that in some areas U.S. students outstrip the students of all other nations. This book will not show, although it could, that the presence of standards in other countries is a very mixed bag. But the importance of Spillane's comment lies not in the accuracy of its content but in the accuracy with which it captures the *Zeitgeist* concerning standards: our kids need to learn more and standards are the way to get there.

We shall see.

References

Berliner, D., and B. Biddle. (1995). *The Manufactured Crisis: Myths, Fraud, and the Attack on America's Public Schools*. Reading, Mass.: Addison-Wesley.

Bestor, A. (1953). *Educational Wastelands: The Retreat from Learning in Public Schools*. Champaign, Ill.: University of Illinois Press.

Bracey, G. (1995). *Final Exam: A Study of the Perpetual Scrutiny of American Education*. Bloomington, Ind.: TECHNOS Press of the Agency for Instructional Technology.

"Crisis in Education." (March 24, 1958). *Life*, pp. 25–35.

Jennings, J.F. (1996). *The Good—And the Not So Good—News About American Schools*. Washington, D.C.: National Center for Education Policy.

Lawton, M. (August 7, 1996). "AFT Report: States Lagging on Standards." *Education Week*, p. 1.

National Commission on Excellence in Education. (April 1983). *A Nation at Risk: A Report to the Nation*. Washington, D.C.: U.S. Government Printing Office.

Rickover, H.G. (1959). *Education and Freedom*. New York: E.P. Dutton.

Spillane, R. (June 2, 1993). "Student Achievement Standards." *Education Week*, p. 36.

Wilson, S. (March 24, 1958). "It's Time to Close Our Circus." *Life*, pp. 36–37.

Wirtz, W., and A. Lapointe. (1982). *Measuring the Quality of Education: A Report on Assessing Educational Progress*. Washington, D.C.: Authors.

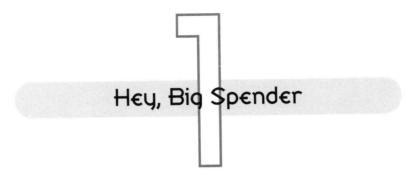

Hey, Big Spender

What do I say when someone says, "The United States spends more money on its public schools than any other nation in the world"?

It is not clear where this myth originated, but it is certainly often repeated. In a long letter to the editor in the October 1993 issue of *Phi Delta Kappan,* Arizona State University professor David Berliner quotes virtually everyone in the Bush administration cabinet as uttering some version of it. "I can find no support for that," says Berliner. Berliner cannot find support because none exists. Nevertheless, people continue to repeat the myth. In *Reinventing Education* (1994), IBM CEO Louis V. Gerstner and his coauthors declare that "[t]otal spending on education in America is without equal in the world." University of Illinois professor Herbert Walberg makes a similar claim in a 1994 newspaper article. When I challenged Walberg in the "Fourth Bracey Report on the Condition of Public Education," Walberg (1995) fired off a letter to the editor pointing to a specific year and a specific page of the *Condition of Public Education.* A check revealed it to be the wrong year and the wrong page; but when the correct reference was located, it did indeed show the United States as number one in the world in spending. But the reference used a peculiar definition of "the world": the United States and five other countries.

In Brief

In brief, you can say the following:

- It's not true. Most calculations place U.S. spending at about the average among developed nations.
- It's only true if higher education is included. College costs a lot, and we send far more of our students to college than any other nation except Canada. Currently, 62 percent of U.S. students who graduate from high school in June are in colleges and universities the following October.

In Detail

Although the computation of how much nations spend on their schools would appear at first to be quite straightforward, it can, in fact, be done a number of ways, each producing somewhat different results. None of the formulas is completely fair to all nations. Some, for instance, do not take into account differences in purchasing power, and others ignore fluctuations in rates of currency exchange. What is telling, however, is that no matter how the computations are performed, no matter what formula is used, the United States never ranks above the average.

Figure 1.1 shows expenditures as a percent of per capita income. As can be seen, the United States ranks 14th among 16 developed nations. Figure 1.2 shows spending simply in terms of U.S. dollars per pupil. Here we rank 9th among 16 countries. The National Center for Education Statistics, in its useful publication *Education in States and Nations* (1993), tried to make these per-pupil expenditures more directly comparable by using a statistic called the Purchasing Power Parity Index (PPPI). This index attempts to show what similar goods and services would cost when purchasing powers of different currencies in different countries are equated. When the index is applied, the United States rises to 6th place among 19 nations of the Organization for Economic Cooperation and Development (OECD).

Various calculations can also measure the commitment a nation has to its educational systems—how much of its wealth it uses to

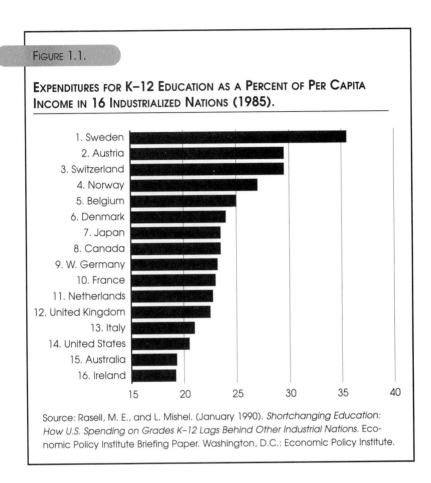

FIGURE 1.1.

EXPENDITURES FOR K–12 EDUCATION AS A PERCENT OF PER CAPITA INCOME IN 16 INDUSTRIALIZED NATIONS (1985).

Source: Rasell, M. E., and L. Mishel. (January 1990). *Shortchanging Education: How U.S. Spending on Grades K–12 Lags Behind Other Industrial Nations.* Economic Policy Institute Briefing Paper. Washington, D.C.: Economic Policy Institute.

educate its citizens. The OECD calculated this in two ways in its publication *Education at a Glance* (1993). Using the gross domestic product (GDP) as an index, the OECD found that the United States ranked 9th among 19 OECD nations (see Figure 1.3 on page 17).[1] Some would object to this calculation on the grounds that nations vary a great deal in the size of their GDP. However, calculating the spending in terms of *per capita* GDP removes this size effect. Such a calculation, shown in Figure 1.4, leaves the U.S. rank unchanged.

---

[1] These nations are Australia, Austria, Canada, Denmark, Finland, France, Ireland, Italy, Japan, Luxembourg, Netherlands, Norway, Portugal, Spain, Sweden, Switzerland, United Kingdom, United States and Germany (the former West Germany).

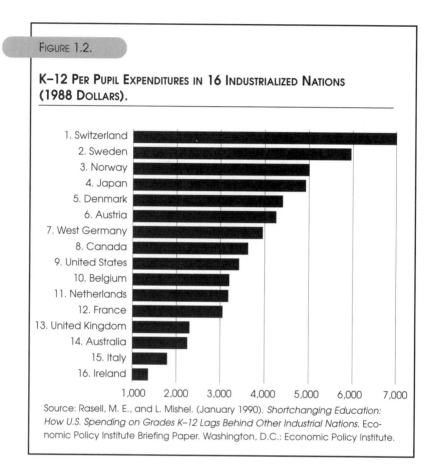

FIGURE 1.2.

K–12 PER PUPIL EXPENDITURES IN 16 INDUSTRIALIZED NATIONS (1988 DOLLARS).

Source: Rasell, M. E., and L. Mishel. (January 1990). *Shortchanging Education: How U.S. Spending on Grades K–12 Lags Behind Other Industrial Nations.* Economic Policy Institute Briefing Paper. Washington, D.C.: Economic Policy Institute.

The rankings shown in Figures 1.3 and 1.4 are misleading, however, because fewer school budget dollars get into the classroom in the United States than in other countries. Former Secretary of Education William Bennett declared that U.S. schools are being smothered by an "administrative blob." However, as shown in Chapter 14, U.S. schools are quite lean compared with other sectors of the economy. Fewer dollars in U.S. school budgets reach the classroom because they go for services that other nations either do not provide or that they provide in reduced amounts. For example, many countries have no transportation budgets either because neighborhood schools are the rule or because the children use regular public trans-

FIGURE 1.3.

SCHOOL SPENDING AS A PERCENT OF GROSS DOMESTIC PRODUCT (1988).

Nation	Percent of GDP
1. Denmark	4.6
2. Finland	4.6
3. Sweden	4.6
4. Luxembourg	4.5
5. Norway	4.4
6. Ireland	4.3
7. Canada	3.8
8. Switzerland	3.7
9. UNITED STATES	3.7
10. France	3.5
11. Portugal	3.5
12. United Kingdom	3.4
13. Italy	3.4
14. Netherlands	3.1
15. Spain	3.0
16. Australia	2.9
17. Austria	2.9
18. West Germany	2.6
19. Japan	2.5

Source: NCES. (1993). *Education in the States and Nations.* Washington, D.C.: Author.

portation services. Also, families in most other nations are responsible for food. Most importantly, U.S. school funds over the past 25 years have been increasingly allotted to special education services, a phenomenon dealt with in Chapter 18.

Although the dollar figures cited in this chapter are several years old, more recent figures released as this book was going to press indicate that the situation has changed little in recent years (see Appendix A).

FIGURE 1.4.

PUBLIC SPENDING ON EDUCATION AS PERCENT OF PER CAPITA GROSS DOMESTIC PRODUCT (1988).

Nation	Percent of GDP
1. Sweden	30.0
2. Luxembourg	28.6
3. Denmark	25.9
4. Finland	25.8
5. Switzerland	25.4
6. Norway	23.2
7. Canada	20.5
8. Austria	19.7
9. UNITED STATES	19.6
10. Italy	19.0
11. Portugal	18.8
12. United Kingdom	17.3
13. Ireland	16.6
14. France	15.6
15. Australia	15.5
16. West Germany	15.1
17. Netherlands	14.5
18. Japan	13.2
19. Spain	12.8

Source: NCES. (1993). *Education in the States and Nations.* Washington, D.C.: Author.

In Sum

When someone says that the United States spends more money on its schools than any other nation, you can respond that this is true only if higher education is included. Colleges in the United States are expensive, and 62 percent of our high school graduates enroll in college the fall after graduation. If we limit our perspectives to elementary and secondary schools and calculate expenditures as a percent of per capita income, as a proportion of GDP, as a proportion of per capita GDP, or in terms of per pupil expenditures, the United States never finishes better than average among the 20 or so developed nations. And even that average ranking is misleading. Because the United States provides services that other countries either don't provide or provide to a lesser extent (namely food, transportation, counseling, and—especially—special education), fewer dollars of the school budget actually get into the classroom. Special education alone accounts for more than one-third of the new money spent on education in the last 25 years.

References

Berliner, D. (October 1993). "The Author Responds." *Phi Delta Kappan* 75, 2: 193.

Gerstner, L.V. Jr., R.D. Semerat, D.P. Doyle, and W.B. Johnston. (1994). *Reinventing Education*. New York: Dutton.

National Center for Education Statistics. (1993). *Education in States and Nations*. (Report No. NCES 93–237). Washington, D.C.: U.S. Department of Education.

Organization for Economic Cooperation and Development. (1993). *Education at a Glance*. Paris: Author.

Walberg, H. (February 1995). "Stands by Statement." *Phi Delta Kappan* 76, 6: 503

Throwing Money at the Schools

What do I say when someone says, "Money doesn't matter. Don't throw money at the schools"?

"We can't solve education's problems by throwing money at the schools." This is one of the most common statements made in defense of withholding resources from school districts. The principal source of this comment is a study conducted by University of Rochester professor Eric Hanushek and reported in the May 1989 issue of the *Educational Researcher.* In his article, Hanushek claimed that he had analyzed the results of 187 studies relating money and outcomes by using the econometric technique of analyzing "production functions." He concluded that "there is no strong or systematic relationship between money and achievement" (p. 47). Because this statement fit so well with the Reagan and Bush education agenda, it was widely cited by those in office at the time.

More recently, former Secretary of Education William Bennett (1993) conducted an analysis relating state spending on schools to state-level SAT scores and concluded there was no relationship. This was a dishonest act on Bennett's part, and it is discouraging that it should be made by the author of *The Book of Virtues.* As we shall see below, Bennett used figures that he knew were misleading.

In Brief

In brief, you can say the following:

- Hanushek's own data contradict Hanushek's conclusion that no strong relationship links money and achievement.
- Bennett's study, which found no relationship between state spending and state-level SAT scores, is an exercise in hypocrisy.
- Well-conducted, honest studies have found that, indeed, money is related to achievement.

In Detail

Because Bennett's study is so readily dismissed, let us scatter it to the winds first. Bennett used state-level SAT scores as his measure of achievement and per-pupil expenditures at the state levels as his measure of spending. Let us note at the beginning that both the College Board, sponsor of the SAT, and Educational Testing Service, developer of the SAT, have long contended that the SAT is *not* a measure of achievement, is *not* a measure of school outcomes. But for the moment, let's accept Bennett's contention that it is; his study still falls apart. Bennett merely noted that many of the low-spending states have high SAT scores and some of the high-spending ones do not. Pundit and fellow ideologue George Will (August 26, 1993) pounced on Bennett's finding and trumpeted it in one of his *Washington Post* columns. Will observed that the top five states in terms of SAT scores—Iowa, North Dakota, South Dakota, Utah, and Minnesota—were all low spenders. On the other hand, New Jersey spent more money per student per year than any other state in the nation and still finished only 39th in the great SAT race.

What neither Will nor Bennett bothered to observe, of course, was that in those high-scoring states, virtually no one takes the SAT. In the year of the study, the percentage of high school seniors taking the SAT was 5 percent in Iowa, 6 percent in North Dakota, 5 percent in South Dakota, 4 percent in Utah, and 10 percent in Minnesota. The rest of the college-bound seniors in these states are not dumb. They take the other college entrance examination battery, the ACT. Those taking the SAT are those interested in attending such institutions as Stanford and the Ivy League and Seven Sisters colleges, which require the SAT.

In New Jersey, on the other hand, fully 76 percent of the senior class huddled in angst on Saturday mornings to bubble in answer sheets on the SAT. We could applaud New Jersey for encouraging three-quarters of its senior class to apply to schools that require the SAT. But, of course, when a team composed of 75 percent of the class goes up against a team made up of a 5 percent elite, the elite will always win the day.

Pundit Will might not have known about the different participation rates in different states, but Bennett certainly did. When Terrel Bell, Bennett's predecessor, was secretary of education, he instituted the release of state-level rankings on many variables in what came to be called the "wall charts." Bennett continued the practice. But under both Bell and Bennett, the wall charts divided states into two categories before ranking them: SAT states and ACT states. Thus Bennett knew that the SAT was not a valid measure for all states.

A study by Powell and Steelman (November 1984), likely also known to Bennett, showed that most of the variation in scores among states is due to the participation factor. The authors recently published another study (Spring 1996) showing, once again, that 85 percent of the differences among the states in SAT scores is due to differences in the proportion of seniors taking the test. This time, however, the authors went a bit further and statistically adjusted the proportions to equate them. They found that if all states had the same participation rate, SAT scores increased 15 points for every $1,000 spent above the national average. Thus, even on an outcome so tangentially related to the classroom, money makes a difference.

Hanushek's study is flawed in a number of ways. Two reanalyses of the same data have shown that Hanushek's data contradict Hanushek's conclusions. Independent researcher Keith Baker (1991) pointed out that although Hanushek claimed to have reviewed 187 studies, only 65 actually dealt with the money-achievement relationship. More importantly, although Hanushek *stated* that that there was no relationship between money and achievement, he did not explain the "decision rule" that he used to reach his conclusion. He simply presented the numbers and concluded that no relationship exists.

When Baker established some reasonable decision rules to reach a conclusion, he found that many more studies indicated a positive relationship than indicated no relationship. Of the 65 studies, 38 indicated a positive relationship and 14 indicated a negative relationship (the rest either found no relationship or did not present enough data to allow a conclusion one way or another).

Baker also noticed an important flaw in Hanushek's logic. Hanushek's analysis dealt with the *level* of achievement that students attained, but his recommendation not to throw money at the schools dealt with *changes* in achievement. As Baker pointed out, these are two very different variables in terms of what affects them. *Level* of achievement is affected greatly by nonschool variables—family and community variables. A recent study by Educational Research Service researchers (Robinson and Brandon 1994) found that most of the differences among states in level of achievement were attributable to four nonschool variables: parental education level, number of parents in the home, type of community, and state-level poverty rates for ages 5 through 17. This is not to say that schools are unimportant, but to say that family and community variables are typically more important in determining *level* of achievement.

Baker pointed out, however, that *changes* in levels of achievement appear to be much less affected by nonschool variables. Thus, if we put more money into an impoverished inner-city school, we might well expect to see changes in achievement, although the level of achievement in the school would not rise to levels attained in more affluent neighborhoods.

Baker also observed that Hanushek's methodology was primitive. Baker suggested that someone should conduct a "meta-analysis" on the data. At the time, meta-analysis was a recently developed quantitative technique for combining many different studies and arriving at a single number that indicated what had or had not been found. Several years after Baker's recommendation, researchers at the University of Chicago conducted a meta-analysis of the studies Hanushek had reviewed and found a large effect size—that is, money is strongly related to achievement (Hedges, Laine, and Greenwald 1994).

Finally, Baker concluded that his finding was a cause for shame. It meant that we were underfunding poor districts. "Think about hospital costs and dead patients," Baker wrote.

> We would not be surprised to find that patients who die cost more in medical care than those who are cured. Indeed, policy makers guarantee this outcome by making every effort to prolong life. . . . A good school resembles a good hospital in that more resources are devoted to treating those who are most difficult to deal with—the sickest patients or the least able students. . . . A positive relationship between spending and achievement indicates a failure of the education system to adequately address the needs of disadvantaged students (p. 629).

We can note here that in some countries, Baker's recommended relationship can be found: poor school districts receive two to three times the amount of money as affluent districts. In this country, the reverse holds.

It is common to search for the relationship between money and achievement by taking one measure of each and calculating a correlation coefficient. This technique is often misleading however, because of what statisticians call "restriction of range." This restriction of range is easily illustrated. Imagine that you are the dean of admissions at a college and you want to use SAT scores to predict success in college. This would be done by correlating SAT scores with, say, freshman grade point averages. But imagine further that in one year all the students had the identical SAT score. In this case the range is completely restricted: everyone looks just alike, and because they are identical in their SATs, the SAT cannot be used to make differential predictions about their success in school. It's as though you wanted to predict success in basketball using height, and everyone who showed up was six-feet-two-inches tall.

Spending ranges are often restricted, particularly when dealing with district-level spending. Whereas the highest-spending districts in a state typically spend two to four times as much as the lowest-spending districts, most districts spend very similar amounts, and this restricts the range: most districts look alike.

Even given this caution, the proper measure can produce a correlation. The SAT is not a proper measure because of the varying proportions of students in various states who take the SAT. The National Assessment of Educational Progress (NAEP), on the other hand, is administered to a representative sample in all participating schools. Howard Wainer (1993) at Educational Testing Service correlated NAEP scores with spending and found a definite relationship. Said Wainer, "My goal here was merely to indicate that the NAEP rankings are a more suitable dependent variable [than SAT rankings] for such comparisons, and that even the grossest possible kind of comparison shows the spending money is related to higher scores" (p. 24).

At the Alabama Department of Education, Robert Lockwood and James McLean (1993) found that those districts that spent more money for instructional materials had higher test scores. And Ronald Ferguson (1991) of Harvard found that districts that used money to reduce class size or to lure teachers with more experience also had rising test scores.

Obviously, if the district superintendent uses extra money as a jobs program for a few cousins, a rise in test scores might not occur. Schools, like individuals, can waste money as well as spend it wisely. As noted in Chapter 1, in order to know what to expect from extra money, we have to know where the money went.

Still, the overwhelming bulk of evidence indicates that money matters. We can see the rationality and truth of this statement if we imagine spending going to extremes. If we spent zero dollars per pupil per year, surely achievement would plummet. This happened in Prince Edward County, Virginia, which closed its schools for a time rather than integrate them. At the other end, imagine that we spent $37,000 a year on each student. Surely achievement would soar. Thirty-seven thousand dollars is not an arbitrary figure, but the amount of money the average teacher currently makes in a year. With such a sum we could hire a teacher—a tutor—for each child. Tutoring has been shown to produce dramatic increases in achievement.

In Sum

When someone says, "Money doesn't matter," you can respond, "It certainly does!" Two groups using sophisticated research techniques found that even the study cited most frequently to supposedly show that money and achievement are not related actually shows that they are. William Bennett's study correlating state-level SAT scores and state-level spending is easily dismissed because the proportion of students taking the SAT varies from 4 percent in Utah to 82 percent in Connecticut. When this differential participation rate is taken into account, states that spend more money are revealed to have higher SAT scores.

Moreover, other studies have found correlations between money spent and test scores. For example, a correlation exists between state-level spending and state-level NAEP scores. School districts that spend more money on instructional materials have higher test scores. And districts that use money to attract experienced teachers or to reduce class size have rising test scores (the class-size phenomenon, however, applies only when class sizes are significantly reduced—in the research cited, to 19 or below).

Studies that simply correlate district spending with test scores are affected by "restriction of range." Although the wealthiest districts in a state spend three to four times as much as the poorest, most districts spend a very similar amount of money. This similarity in spending makes it hard to see the impact of money.

Certainly, if spending dropped to zero, achievement would plummet. If spending rose to $37,000 a year—enough to provide each student with a full-time tutor—achievement would soar.

References

Baker, K. (April 1991). "Yes, Throw Money at the Schools." *Phi Delta Kappan* 72, 8: 628–630.

Bennett, W. (1993). "Report Card on American Education." Washington, D.C.: American Legislative Exchange Council.

Ferguson, R. (1991)."Paying for Public Education: New Evidence on How and Why Money Matters." *Harvard Journal on Legislation* 28, 2: 465–498.

Hanushek, E. (May 1989). "The Impact of Differential School Expenditures on School Performance." *Educational Researcher* 18, 4:45–51.

Hedges, L.V., R. D. Laine, and R. Greenwald. (April 1994). "Does Money Matter? A Meta-Analysis of Studies of the Effects of Differential School Inputs on Student Outcomes. *Educational Researcher* 24, 3: 5–14.

Lockwood, R., and J. McLean. (November 10–12, 1993). "Educational Funding and Student Achievement." Paper presented at the Mid-South Educational Research Association, New Orleans.

Powell, B., and L.C. Steelman. (Fall 1984). "Variations in State SAT Scores: Meaningful or Misleading?" *Harvard Educational Review* 54, 4: 389–412.

Powell, B., and L.C. Steelman. (Spring 1996). "Bewitched, Bothered and Bewildering: The Use and Misuse of State SAT Scores." *Harvard Educational Review* 66, 1: 29–59.

Robinson, G., and D. Brandon. (1994). "NAEP Test Scores: Should They Be Used to Compare and Rank State Educational Quality?" (Stock #0182). Arlington, Va: Educational Research Service.

Wainer, H. (December 1993). "Does Spending Money on Education Help?" *Educational Researcher* 23, 10: 22–24.

Will, G. (August 26, 1993). "Meaningless Money Factor." *Washington Post,* p. C7.

Rising Costs, Flat Scores

What do I say when someone says, "During the 1980s, expenditures for public education rose by 34 percent (in real dollars), but test scores were static," or when someone says, "In the last 25 years, spending on public schools has risen by 100 percent, but test scores are flat"?

These are common statements. The first was uttered by, among others, Hudson Institute consultant and now Heritage Foundation fellow Denis Doyle in 1992 and repeated in the book he co-authored with IBM CEO Louis V. Gerstner Jr. and two RJR executives in 1994, *Reinventing Education.* (Gerstner headed RJR during the height of its "Joe Camel" ad campaign; one wonders how committed to our youth cigarette executives can actually be, since kids who understand the effects of smoking won't buy their products.) The latter statement was made by, among others, University of Rochester education economist Eric Hanushek, and by former Assistant Secretary of Education Chester E. Finn Jr. at a November 1994 Brookings Institution luncheon launching Hanushek's book on education reform (a book whose arguments are based on the false assumption dealt with in Chapter 2).

In Brief

In brief, you can say the following:

• Spending has not gone up nearly as much as critics contend.

• Increased spending has gone principally for special education and other programs for special populations: there would be little reason to expect increases in test scores from such increases in spending.

• Despite the second point above, test scores have been rising since the mid-1970s. They are, indeed, currently flat, but they are flat *at record highs.*

In Detail

The contention that spending on education has risen 100 percent in the last 25 years comes from using the consumer price index (CPI) as an indicator of inflation and adjusting the calculation of expenditures accordingly. Using the CPI, expenditures have, indeed, gone up by 100 percent in the last quarter century.

However, a recent study by Richard Rothstein and Karen Hawley Miles of the Economic Policy Institute (1995) argues that the CPI is not an appropriate index of inflation for education. The CPI is useful in calculating changes in the price of *commodities,* but far less so for calculating changes in *services,* especially the kind of service industry represented by schools. One could argue that even for some service-intensive industries, the CPI is acceptable as a measure of price changes and as a productivity index. Telecommunications is a good example. Telecommunications has recently realized big improvements in productivity through automation. Banking, through the use of ATMs, has seen similar improvements in productivity. But while technology might one day offer such improvements in education, to date it has not.

Rothstein and Miles take these factors into account and calculate what they call the Net Services Index. The index finds that over the last 25 years spending on education has increased 61 percent.

In any case, technology is more likely to affect businesses that use *things* rather than activities such as education. Education resembles a symphony orchestra more than it resembles a product industry. How can a symphony increase productivity? It cannot do so by playing the same music faster each year or by playing it with fewer players. Actually, schools *could* play with fewer players by increasing the pupil/teacher ratio, but as we will see in an answer to another question, this gain in productivity in one place is offset by losses elsewhere: with higher pupil/teacher ratios, achievement goes down. This outcome is much like a barber increasing his productivity by shaving customers at an ever faster pace. More people are going to get cut.

The quotes that opened this chapter make simplistic contentions. Nevertheless, their simplistic nature must be pointed out and dealt with. To know whether money should have any effect on test scores, we must know not just that money for schools has increased, but also where the money has gone. As Rothstein and Miles (1995) put it,

> To understand school spending and to determine whether school productivity is truly declining (i.e., whether additional dollars have been well used), expenditures must be linked to the program and to the specific outcomes the spending was designed to enhance. If, for example, schools have used much of their new money to improve the training of mentally handicapped youngsters, it would make no sense to judge the effectiveness of this spending by whether SAT scores improved for the college bound (p. 8).

Two studies at the state and local levels provide an answer to the "where has the money gone?" question. Both found that much of the money has gone to special education. Hamilton Lankford and James Wyckoff (1993) at the State University of New York examined this issue for the state of New York. They found that special education accounted for 5.9 percent of school expenditures in the state in 1980. But by 1992 special education's share had soared to 13.1 percent, a 122 percent increase. Increases in spending for special education accounted for 26 percent of all increases from 1980 to 1989 and *85 percent* of all increases from 1989 to 1992.

In a similar analysis (Carson, Huelskamp, and Woodall 1993), engineers from Sandia National Laboratories discovered that in Albuquerque, New Mexico, the costs of regular education increased by only 8 percent from 1976 to 1990, while the costs for special education had skyrocketed by 340 percent. Both the New York and New

Mexico analyses reached similar conclusions: little of the additional money spent on education found its way into regular classrooms.

At the national level, Rothstein and Miles (1995) uncovered similar trends. In 1967 special education received only 4 percent of all spending, while in 1991 it received 17 percent, a 325 percent increase. It accounted for fully 38 percent of all new spending in that period. Other increases went for dropout programs and breakfast and lunch programs. Regular education got less than a quarter of the increases in school spending from 1967 to 1991.

As a minor aside, none of these studies finds any evidence for former Secretary of Education William Bennett's invention, "the administrative blob." All of them find administrative costs little changed over the periods examined. And, as shown in Chapter 14, schools are very lean compared with many other industries in terms of the ratio of frontline employees to supervisors. Compared with the industry average, schools have twice as many frontline employees per supervisor.

As for test scores being "flat," Figures 3.1, 3.2, and 3.3 show that they have been anything but. Figures 3.1 and 3.3 show changes in the Iowa Tests of Basic Skills (ITBS) from 1955 to 1992 in grades 3 through 8, and Figure 3.2 depicts the changes in the Iowa Tests of Educational Development (ITED) from 1962 to 1990 in grades 9 through 12. As all three figures indicate, test scores started to decline in most grades around 1965 and fell for a decade or so before beginning to rise steadily, attaining record levels around 1988 and maintaining them ever since.

You have probably noticed that Figures 3.1 and 3.2 present data from Iowa only and might wonder why we put them in here. After all, not many states have the same population makeup as Iowa. That is part of the point: demographically, Iowa has changed very little over the years. It is still 97 percent white and largely a farm state. Its largest city, Des Moines, has only about 250,000 inhabitants, and the two next largest cities have only about 125,000 each. These cities have some urban problems, to be certain, but nothing like those of the nation's large urban areas.

For many states, changes in test scores over such a long period of time as represented here would be hard to interpret because so many other things have changed as well. Many states have become

31

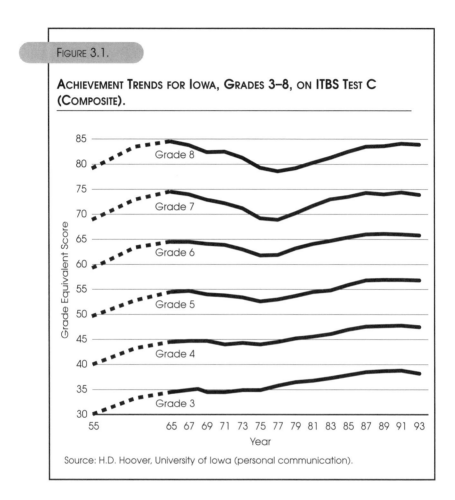

FIGURE 3.1.

ACHIEVEMENT TRENDS FOR IOWA, GRADES 3–8, ON ITBS TEST C (COMPOSITE).

Source: H.D. Hoover, University of Iowa (personal communication).

much more urbanized, while others have experienced large influxes of immigrants from Southeast Asia, or Central and South America, or all three. Iowa's relatively static demography makes it easier to link test scores with what is happening in schools.

In addition, after the emergence of testing's "Lake Wobegon effect," some people have found test scores less credible than previously. Lake Wobegon is a mythical Minnesota town invented by radio host Garrison Keillor for storytelling purposes on his weekly show, "Prairie Home Companion." In Lake Wobegon, "all the women are strong, all the men are good-looking, and all the children are above average." That's fine for Lake Wobegon, but not for a norm-

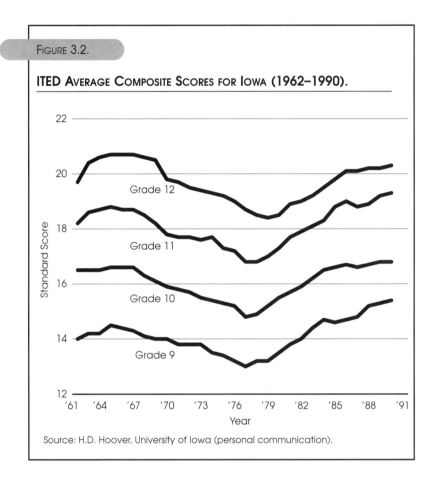

FIGURE 3.2.

ITED AVERAGE COMPOSITE SCORES FOR IOWA (1962–1990).

Source: H.D. Hoover, University of Iowa (personal communication).

referenced achievement test such as the ITBS or ITED. For achievement tests such as these, half of the children, by definition, should be below average. This is how the "norm" of a norm-referenced test is defined. But studies have found that far more than 50 percent of students taking standardized tests are above average. People thus charge that as testing has become more and more a "high stakes" operation, "curriculum alignment" or "teaching to the test" or even outright cheating have been used to increase scores artificially. In some instances this has been true, and as a consequence, many people express skepticism about the credibility of test scores.

But educators pay little attention to these tests in Iowa, at least in terms of getting anxious about them or feeling pressure to get the

33

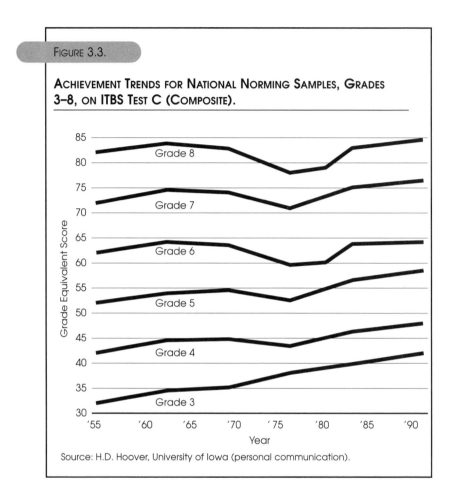

FIGURE 3.3.

ACHIEVEMENT TRENDS FOR NATIONAL NORMING SAMPLES, GRADES 3–8, ON ITBS TEST C (COMPOSITE).

Source: H.D. Hoover, University of Iowa (personal communication).

scores up. The Iowa testing program has been around since the 1930s. It causes no anxieties. In addition, Iowa looks good on whatever test people throw at it, including those where teaching to the test is hard or impossible: the SAT, ACT, and National Assessment of Educational Progress. In fact, Iowa's percentile ranks on the NAEP are almost precisely the same as those on the ITBS! Iowans' performance is a source of pride, not anxiety. Thus, many people find the trend lines in Iowa credible.

It is significant, then, to observe that the curves in Figure 3.3 look just like the curves in Iowa. They are not as smooth, but other than that they are virtually identical. This is crucially important because these curves are *not* from Iowa; they come from national norming studies. They are not as smooth as those from Iowa because test publishers can afford to do national norming studies only every five years or so, whereas the data from Iowa come in annually.

To conduct a national norming study, test publishers try to find a total of about 200,000 students at the various grade levels, so chosen that they are representative of the nation as a whole in terms of ethnicity, type of community, socioeconomic status, and other demographic variables. Only by obtaining such a representative sample can a test publisher meaningfully speak about a "national norm."

One other point should be made about the ITBS and ITED: because of a state law, these tests are equated from form to form as each new form appears. This is important because it is what makes the 40-year trends in the figures meaningful. For most tests, the standards are floating: when each new edition is normed, the average score in each curriculum area becomes the national norm; and this average score might well fluctuate from time to time. In one norming sample, the average might be 19 out of 40 items right, and in another 22 out of 40.

Although long-term analyses with other tests are more difficult, they can be done. Figure 3.4 shows the average yearly gains in reading and mathematics during the 1980s for a variety of tests. As the figure indicates, while the gains on the Iowa tests were sufficient to take the scores to record levels, some tests have registered even larger gains.

In sum, the fact that national norming trend lines look the same as those very credible lines from Iowa indicates that scores in the country as a whole have shown authentic increases as well.

The curves in Figures 3.1, 3.2, and 3.3 take on added significance when they are matched against the data appearing in Figure 3.5. These data show the Index of Social Health, created in 1970 at Fordham University's Institute for Innovation in Social Policy (1995). The index combines 17 indicators (such as infant mortality and teen suicide) into a single index that can assume values from 0 to 100.[1] Higher scores indicate better social health.

---

[1] The 17 variables are rates of: infant mortality, child abuse, children in poverty, teen suicide, drug abuse, high school dropouts, average weekly earnings, unemployment, health insurance coverage, elderly in poverty, health insurance for elderly, highway death due to alcohol, homicides, food stamp coverage, housing, gap between rich and poor.

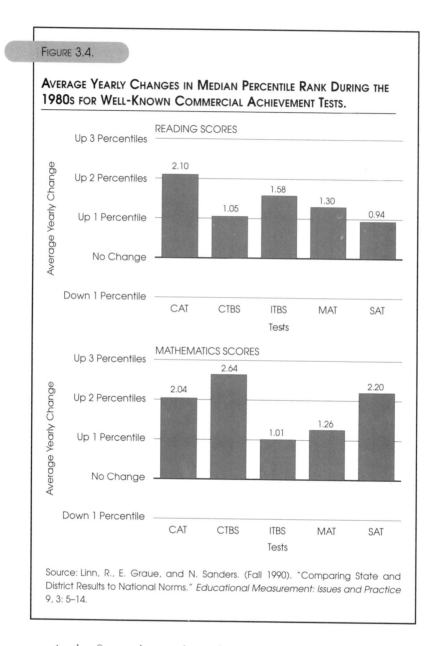

FIGURE 3.4.

AVERAGE YEARLY CHANGES IN MEDIAN PERCENTILE RANK DURING THE 1980S FOR WELL-KNOWN COMMERCIAL ACHIEVEMENT TESTS.

READING SCORES

Up 3 Percentiles

Up 2 Percentiles — 2.10

1.58

Up 1 Percentile — 1.05   1.30   0.94

No Change

Down 1 Percentile

CAT   CTBS   ITBS   MAT   SAT

Tests

Average Yearly Change

MATHEMATICS SCORES

Up 3 Percentiles — 2.64

Up 2 Percentiles — 2.04   2.20

Up 1 Percentile — 1.01   1.26

No Change

Down 1 Percentile

CAT   CTBS   ITBS   MAT   SAT

Tests

Average Yearly Change

Source: Linn, R., E. Graue, and N. Sanders. (Fall 1990). "Comparing State and District Results to National Norms." *Educational Measurement: Issues and Practice* 9, 3: 5–14.

As the figure shows, the index attains its highest score about 1973 and then starts a steep decline *just as test scores end their decline and start back up!* The index has remained at low levels since beginning its decline, while test scores have continued to increase.

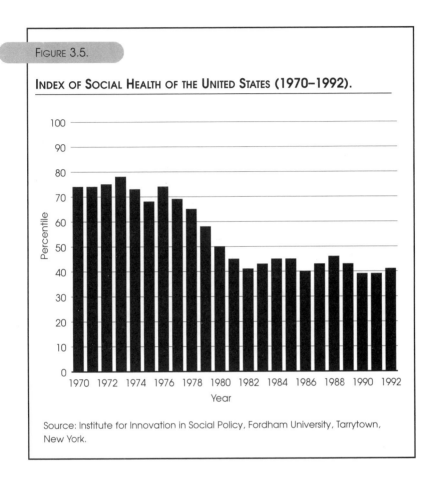

FIGURE 3.5.

INDEX OF SOCIAL HEALTH OF THE UNITED STATES (1970–1992).

Source: Institute for Innovation in Social Policy, Fordham University, Tarrytown, New York.

Some people view the increase in test scores at a time when social institutions are declining as, well, amazing.

Before we conclude the discussion of achievement tests, one other matter is worth addressing. You may have noticed an intriguing change in the curves in Figures 3.1 and 3.3 as we come up the grade ladder: grade 3 shows only the barest hint of any decline in test scores, but a more pronounced decline characterizes each succeeding grade level. Many explanations have been put forward for the decline, but none for why it affects upper grades more than lower ones. In looking at the declines in the SAT—occurring at the same time—the committee appointed by the College Board (1977) to examine the decline referred to this period as "a decade of distraction." It noted the Vietnam War,

Watergate, the riot at the 1968 Democratic convention in Chicago, urban unrest, the civil rights movement, the women's movement, and other manifestations of civil discontent. Some have alleged that teachers entering the force during this period were not as well prepared as previous teachers, but this is hard to verify. In any case, they would constitute only a small proportion of the teaching force each year.

Others have contended that the dreadful curriculums developed after *Sputnik* was launched in 1957 are the culprits. Educators held out much hope for these curriculums. They were developed by some of the finest minds at our universities, after all. But in the end this turned out to be their greatest weakness: the developers were excellent mathematicians and scientists, but they were isolated on university campuses, remote from the history of curriculum development and from the dynamics of the classroom. The goal of these curriculum makers was to make the materials "teacher proof." As a consequence, they produced materials that were irrelevant.

Despite these various speculations, the question as to why declines in achievement tests were steeper in upper grades than in lower grades remains largely unresolved. No one has provided a definite—much less a definitive—answer.

Looking at the National Assessment of Educational Progress (NAEP), the curves do not show the same up-and-down trends as the commercial achievement tests. For the most part, they have been slowly rising since NAEP's inception in 1969. It is not clear why the curves for NAEP look different from the curves for achievement tests, but it is quite possibly because no one takes NAEP seriously. NAEP, when it comes, arrives one day, disappears the same day, and never returns. The students don't know their scores, the teachers don't know, the principals don't know, the central administration doesn't know, and the school board doesn't know. When I worked in a district that participated in a NAEP program, I called all the teachers to a meeting to debrief me on what had transpired. About half said they had trouble keeping the kids on task.

Incidentally, the authors of *A Nation at Risk* (National Commission on Excellence in Education, April 1983) used NAEP in the selective way that they used much data. Listing the reasons why we were a nation at risk, the authors wrote, "There was a steady decline in the science achievement of 17-year-olds as measured by NAEP in 1969, 1973, and 1977" (p. 9). This statement is true. But when a statement that purports to be a general conclusion is qualified in important ways, suspicions should be aroused. Why did they pick on science? And why did they pick on 17-year-olds? The answer is given in Figures 3.6, 3.7, and 3.8. These graphs show that of the nine trends mea-

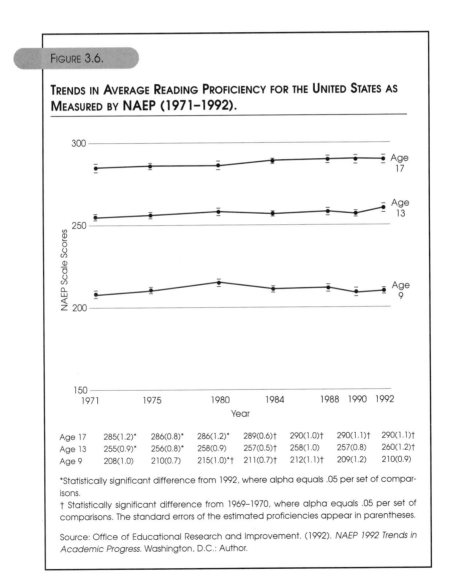

FIGURE 3.6.

TRENDS IN AVERAGE READING PROFICIENCY FOR THE UNITED STATES AS MEASURED BY NAEP (1971–1992).

	285(1.2)*	286(0.8)*	286(1.2)*	289(0.6)†	290(1.0)†	290(1.1)†	290(1.1)†
Age 17	285(1.2)*	286(0.8)*	286(1.2)*	289(0.6)†	290(1.0)†	290(1.1)†	290(1.1)†
Age 13	255(0.9)*	256(0.8)*	258(0.9)	257(0.5)†	258(1.0)	257(0.8)	260(1.2)†
Age 9	208(1.0)	210(0.7)	215(1.0)*†	211(0.7)†	212(1.1)†	209(1.2)	210(0.9)

*Statistically significant difference from 1992, where alpha equals .05 per set of comparisons.
† Statistically significant difference from 1969–1970, where alpha equals .05 per set of comparisons. The standard errors of the estimated proficiencies appear in parentheses.

Source: Office of Educational Research and Improvement. (1992). *NAEP 1992 Trends in Academic Progress.* Washington, D.C.: Author.

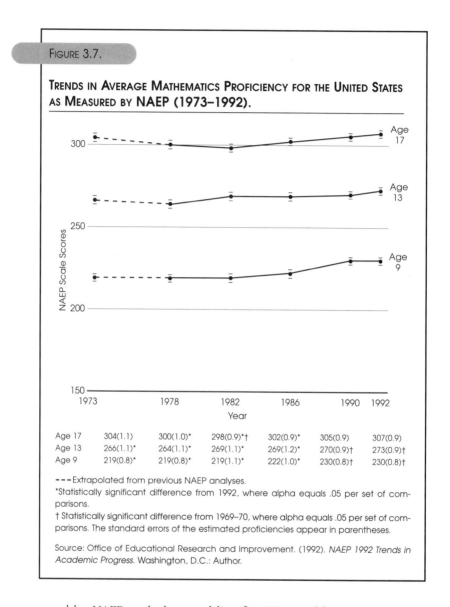

FIGURE 3.7.

TRENDS IN AVERAGE MATHEMATICS PROFICIENCY FOR THE UNITED STATES AS MEASURED BY NAEP (1973–1992).

	1973	1978	1982	1986	1990	1992
Age 17	304(1.1)	300(1.0)*	298(0.9)*†	302(0.9)*	305(0.9)	307(0.9)
Age 13	266(1.1)*	264(1.1)*	269(1.1)*	269(1.2)*	270(0.9)†	273(0.9)†
Age 9	219(0.8)*	219(0.8)*	219(1.1)*	222(1.0)*	230(0.8)†	230(0.8)†

- - - Extrapolated from previous NAEP analyses.
*Statistically significant difference from 1992, where alpha equals .05 per set of comparisons.
† Statistically significant difference from 1969–70, where alpha equals .05 per set of comparisons. The standard errors of the estimated proficiencies appear in parentheses.

Source: Office of Educational Research and Improvement. (1992). *NAEP 1992 Trends in Academic Progress*. Washington, D.C.: Author.

sured by NAEP, *only* the trend line for 17-year-olds on science supports the contention that schools are in trouble.

In *Final Exam: A Study of the Perpetual Scrutiny of American Education* (Bracey 1995), I showed that the commission that produced *Risk* was not free to objectively examine the data and reach a disinterested conclusion about American schools. They were called

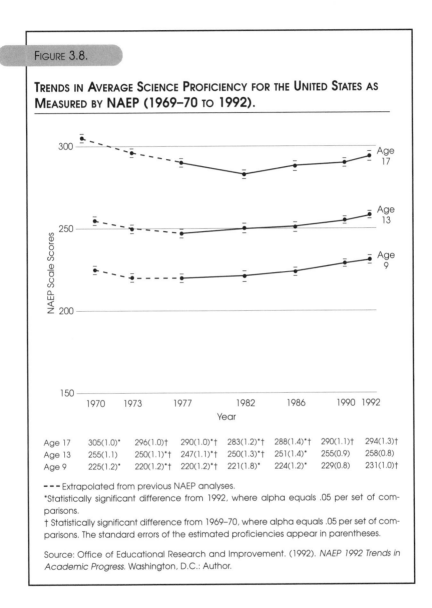

FIGURE 3.8.

TRENDS IN AVERAGE SCIENCE PROFICIENCY FOR THE UNITED STATES AS MEASURED BY NAEP (1969–70 TO 1992).

	1970	1973	1977	1982	1986	1990	1992
Age 17	305(1.0)*	296(1.0)†	290(1.0)*†	283(1.2)*†	288(1.4)*†	290(1.1)†	294(1.3)†
Age 13	255(1.1)	250(1.1)*†	247(1.1)*†	250(1.3)*†	251(1.4)*	255(0.9)	258(0.8)
Age 9	225(1.2)*	220(1.2)*†	220(1.2)*†	221(1.8)*	224(1.2)*	229(0.8)	231(1.0)†

- - - Extrapolated from previous NAEP analyses.
*Statistically significant difference from 1992, where alpha equals .05 per set of comparisons.
† Statistically significant difference from 1969–70, where alpha equals .05 per set of comparisons. The standard errors of the estimated proficiencies appear in parentheses.

Source: Office of Educational Research and Improvement. (1992). *NAEP 1992 Trends in Academic Progress.* Washington, D.C.: Author.

together to *document* all the terrible things that then–Secretary of Education Terrel Bell *knew* were wrong with the system.

The recent flatness of the SATs is largely a function of demographic changes in the student population that has been taking it. Chapter 4 addresses this topic in detail.

In Sum

When someone says school costs keep going up but test scores are flat, you can respond, "They are not!" Test scores fell from about 1965 to 1975, then reversed and have climbed to record highs. In the last decade, all major achievement tests have shown increases almost every year. Gains on NAEP have not been as dramatic, but informal evidence indicates that no one takes NAEP very seriously. Even so, seven of nine NAEP trends in reading, mathematics, and science are at all-time highs. The overall averages of SAT scores have not been rising, but SATs do not reflect well what happens in school. In addition, if we take into account the demographic changes in students taking the SAT, SAT scores are seen to be rising as well.

That test scores have been rising during a period when other social institutions have been declining is a source of some wonderment.

References

Bracey, G. (1995). *Final Exam: A Study of the Perpetual Scrutiny of American Education*. Bloomington, Ind.: Technos Press of the Agency for Instructional Technology.

Carson, C.C., R.M. Huelskamp, and T.D. Woodall. (May/June 1993). "Perspectives on Education in America," *Journal of Educational Research* 86, 5: 261–310.

The College Board. (1977). *On Further Examination: Report of the Advisory Panel on the Scholastic Aptitude Test Score Decline*. New York: Author.

Fordham Institute for Innovation in Social Policy. (1995). *1994 Index of Social Health: Monitoring the Social Well-Being of the Nation*. Tarrytown, N.Y.: Fordham Graduate Center, Fordham University.

Lankford, H., and J. Wyckoff. (Summer 1995). "Where Has the Money Gone?" *Educational Evaluation and Policy Analysis* 17, 2: 195–218.

National Commission on Excellence in Education. (April 1983). *A Nation at Risk: A Report to the Nation*. Washington, D.C.: U.S. Government Printing Office.

Rothstein, R., and K.H. Miles. (1995). *Where's the Money Gone?* Washington, D.C.: Economic Policy Institute.

"Plummeting" SAT Scores

What do I say when someone says, "SAT scores have plummeted"?

People often say this largely because of the way the data are graphed. If the data are graphed on a scale that runs from 400 to 500, then the curves for both the mathematics and verbal sections of the SAT appear to "plunge" or "plummet." Because all of the changes that have occurred in SAT scores since 1963 can be shown using a scale of 100 points, from 400 to 500, the curves are often shown this way. However, each test has a range of 600 points, from 200 to 800. If the entire range of possible scores is shown, the drop looks much less dramatic. A graph should show the entire range of possible scores, but often does not when those preparing the graph want to create a particular impression. For instance, an increase in test scores from the 60th to the 65th percentile looks much more dramatic if the chart begins with the 50th percentile rather than with the 1st percentile.

In Brief

In brief you can say the following:

• SAT scores have changed little since 1951 if the demographic characteristics of those taking the SAT are taken into account. The standards for the SAT were set on the basis of 10,654 students. Ninety-eight percent of them were white, 60 percent were male, and 40 percent were attending private, college preparatory high schools. Currently, 30 percent of SAT takers are minority, 52 percent are women, 88 percent attend public school, and 30 percent report an annual family income of $30,000 or less.

It would not be too flippant to suggest that when someone says, "SAT scores have plummeted," you should respond, "Hooray!" The changes in the population taking the SAT indicate that women and minorities and people of low incomes can aspire to go to those colleges that require the SAT, institutions that for many years were available largely to white males from affluent families. All of these changes are associated, however, with lower SAT scores. It would have been miraculous (and *very* suspicious) if SAT scores *had not* gone down. This is important: there is a major difference between an average that declines because new groups with lower scores are being added into the mix and an average that declines because the same group of students is scoring lower.

In Detail

The SAT was created in 1926, and its creators were quite humble—appropriately—about its capabilities. The principle developer, Carl Campbell Brigham (1926), had this to say about it:

> The present state of all efforts of men to measure or in any way estimate the worth of other men, or to evaluate the results of their nurture, or to reckon their potential possibilities does not warrant any certainty of prediction. . . . This additional test now made available through the instrumentality of the College Entrance Examination Board may help to resolve a few perplexing problems, but it should be regarded merely as a supplementary record. To place too great emphasis on test scores is as dangerous as the failure to properly evaluate any score or rank in conjunction with other measures and estimates which it supplements.

Some of us have argued that the SAT is *so* supplementary that it is useless and shouldn't be bothered with, that it tells colleges nothing they don't already know from the high school record (Crouse and Trusheim 1988; Bracey 1989). In spite of such arguments, the proportion of high school seniors taking the SAT has continued to grow. Forty-three percent of all high school seniors now take the test, and another 35 percent take the ACT (there is some overlap, as some students take both).

When the SAT was created, it replaced the all-essay examinations that the College Board had been administering since its formation in 1900. The multiple-choice format question was invented during World War I, and the board was impressed with the ability of such tests to predict who would become good officers, specialists, and so on. The original SAT incorporated some multiple-choice items along with the traditional essays.

The entry of the United States into World War II interfered with the administration of the essay portion in 1941, and the SAT has been all multiple-choice ever since. It was the elite group described above that set the standards on the SAT. This elite's average raw score was assigned a scaled score of 500 with a standard deviation of 100, giving the SAT its range of 200 to 800 for each of the two sections, verbal (SAT-V) and mathematics (SAT-M).

By 1951 the verbal score had fallen from 500 to 476, and it remained quite stable around 475 until it began its well-publicized slide in 1963. (The math scores suffered no such early decline and hovered around 500 until 1963.) No one has ever addressed this pre-1951 verbal decline, even though it constitutes about one-third of the entire verbal decline. This may be because no one can explain what happened. No major changes in teacher training took place. The only major curriculum development of the time, Life Adjustment Education, could not have affected the test-taking groups, having been conceptualized only in 1945. In any case, Life Adjustment Education was not intended for the college bound. Outside of schools, television had not yet permeated the culture. Families were not only intact, the country was about to enter the "togetherness" years of the Eisenhower administration. In 1951 the country was one year away from a television series that would represent the decade: "Ozzie and Harriet." And only jazz musicians and a few marginalized groups were taking drugs. Thus, not only was there no ferment in schools, the major explanatory outside-of-school variables that would be used later could not be invoked. It might have had something to do with the GI bill, which allowed a group of students to attend college whose finances would have otherwise prevented it. But we will never know.

In 1963, however, the SAT began what would be a 20-year decline. It did not take the full 20 years for people to notice the decline and to start worrying about it. In the early '70s people began to voice alarm as the scores continued to slip. In 1976, the College Board impaneled a group headed by former Secretary of Labor Willard Wirtz and former Commissioner of Education Harold Howe II to look at what was by then a 14-year fall.

The Wirtz panel's report, *On Further Examination* (The College Board 1977), blamed most of the decline up to 1970 on changes in who was taking the test: during these years colleges were accepting more women and were beginning to open their doors to minorities as well. The SAT practice of collecting biographical information from students did not begin until 1972. However, looking at high school records, the panel noted that more and more students with low grade point averages were aspiring to college. The panel claimed, however, that the demographic changes had stabilized by 1972, and so other factors had to be found for the further decline. (Staff to the panel claimed that the demographic changes had *not* stabilized.)

And did the panel find factors! One of its background papers simply listed the hypotheses that had been advanced to explain the decline. There were 79 of them. Even today, many have merit in terms of their plausibility. They cover the entire range of societal, familial, curricular, instructional, and motivational possibilities. Of course, if each hypothesis accounted for only one point of the decline, virtually all of the decline would be accounted for. In addition, the Wirtz panel spoke of a "decade of distraction" (also mentioned in Chapter 3) that included such widely publicized events and major societal changes as the assassinations of John Kennedy, Robert Kennedy, and Martin Luther King Jr.; the civil rights movement; the free speech movement; the riots at the 1968 Democratic national convention in Chicago; the Vietnam War; Watergate; the Watts riots and other urban unrest; and the general "making of a counterculture" that rejected traditional values, including achievement in school. (Many other indicators of achievement declined in this same period.)

Actually, in spite of the Wirtz panel's contention that demographics had stabilized, further demographic changes did take place, changes that were later accelerated by new migrations into the United States of people leaving Southeast Asia, Mexico, and Central and South America. (The number of immigrants legally entering the country each year is now about the same as it was in the peak years just before World War I; this means, of course, that the proportion of immigrants in relation to the proportion of native-born Americans is lower than it was then. We were much more truly a nation of immigrants in the first two decades of this century. Sixty percent of the country's illegal immigrants are people who arrive here legally and overstay their visas; at most, 13 percent of *all* immigrants enter the country illegally.)

The Wirtz panel's report was a major factor in the transformation of the SAT from a "mere supplement" into a platinum rod for measuring the quality of education in the United States. Each minute change of one or two points became annual front-page, prime time news—at least when the scores went down. In recent years the scores have been heading up a bit, and neither the *New York Times* nor the *Washington Post* has given the results the play they gave the downward trends. For the last two years, the *Times* has put its story deep inside the front section, and the *Post* has relegated it to the Metro section, something of only local interest.

In 1990, after reading a column entitled "Johnny's Miserable SATs" by *Post* pundit Richard Cohen, I conducted my own analyses, attempting to control for demographic changes. I found only a 22-point decline since 1951 in the verbal section and a 5-point increase in the mathematics section (Bracey 1990). An analysis with similar intent but different methodology, conducted by engineers at Sandia National Laboratories, reached similar conclusions (Carson, Huelskamp, and Woodall 1993). Had the mix of gender and class rank remained the same from 1975 to 1990, the study found, scores would have risen.

During this same period of 1975–1990, the actual scores of all nonwhite ethnic groups were, in fact, rising.[1] The scores of white students declined slightly. Why, then, was the overall average flat or declining slightly? This result occurred largely because minority students were taking the test in ever increasing numbers. Their scores were on the increase, but still well behind the scores of white students, with the exception of the math scores of Asian Americans. So adding more and more of these low-but-improving scores into the mix dragged the average down or, at best, kept it flat.

The Wirtz panel chose to ignore a major piece of data that contradicted the whole notion of an SAT decline. The panel dealt at some length and repeatedly with the fact that the Preliminary SAT (PSAT) had shown trends similar to those of the SAT. The panel mentioned, then apparently forgot, another PSAT finding: "When the PSAT was given in 1960, again in 1966, and once more in 1974, to national samples of 11th graders as a whole, these 'norming studies' showed a substantial stability in averages on both the Verbal and Mathematical Sections over the entire 14-year period" (The College Board 1977, p. 22). We can add here that a 1983 norming study of the PSAT also found no decline.

So what does this mean? Well, the PSAT is a short version of the SAT. It has some old SAT questions and a few new potential SAT questions that the developers are trying out. The importance of the data reported in the above paragraph is that a norming study represents an attempt on the part of the institution conducting the test to assemble a group of test-takers who are representative of the nation. The SAT test-takers are, on the other hand, not representative of the nation; they are the college-bound segment. At the time of the Wirtz panel, no more than one-third of high school seniors took the test. Moreover, the proportion of seniors showing up on Saturday mornings to take the test varies enormously from state to state, from a low of 4 percent in Utah and Mississippi to a high of 82 percent in Con-

---

[1] Some of us who analyze SAT data by ethnicity have been criticized for beginning our analyses in 1975, when much of the overall decline had already occurred; 1975, however, was the first year that the College Board released data by ethnicity.

necticut. But a norming sample, such as that used for the PSAT norming studies, represents the nation.

This means that the SAT decline can in no way reflect a decline in the verbal and mathematical abilities of the nation's students as a whole. It could be that a real decline took place and it affected only the college bound. This is the case argued by Charles Murray and Richard Herrnstein (1992). They contend that the decline came not from a democratization of the SAT test-taking pool but from the democratization of the college-bound curriculum in high schools. They believe that this opening of the high school college-bound track to more and more people had a devastating impact on high-ability students.

I think that their contention has some merit, but it is not the "devastating" factor that Murray and Herrnstein argue. They do not, for instance, explain how this dumbing down of the college curriculum affected verbal scores but not mathematics scores. And from purely personal experience, I noted that my children were reading much more sophisticated authors and text than I was at a comparable point in high school. The more plausible and more parsimonious explanation still remains the changes in the population taking the SAT.

Figure 4.1 presents the SAT scores over time for whites and various minority groups. Figure 4.2 provides an example of how rising scores for subgroups can still lower the score for the whole group of test-takers.

Even if one accepted the SAT decline as having happened just as the Wirtz panel reported it, one would still have to wonder how significant it was in practical terms. Without even breaking scores out by ethnicity, the SAT test-takers today are getting, on average, about three fewer math questions and six fewer verbal questions correct than their counterparts in 1951. Is this of practical concern? The question is not really answerable.

Should we be concerned if scores start to fall again? Possibly, but it seems unlikely that this will happen in mathematics, and if SAT verbal scores show a further decline, it might not reflect any decline in the quality or rigor of education in general.

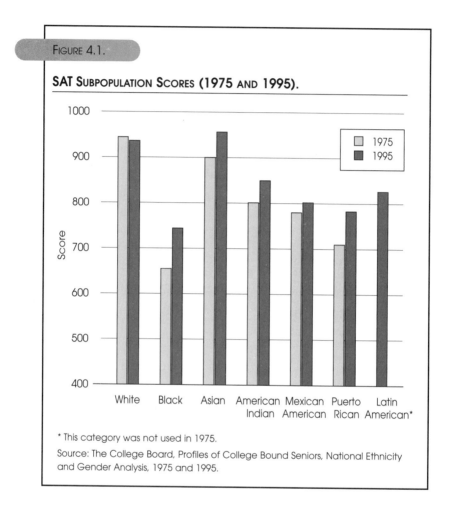

FIGURE 4.1.

SAT SUBPOPULATION SCORES (1975 AND 1995).

* This category was not used in 1975.

Source: The College Board, Profiles of College Bound Seniors, National Ethnicity and Gender Analysis, 1975 and 1995.

The prediction that the SAT-M, at least, will fall no further comes from the fact that since 1982 a larger and larger proportion of students has been taking more and more mathematics courses. This would be important if it did no more than keep students practicing the kinds of skills they need on the math section of the test, for the scores on the math test can be greatly affected by forgetting just a few things learned in 9th grade algebra. For instance, when, as background research for a book review, I took the SAT at the age of 44, I did not review anything for the verbal section. I did not need to, as

FIGURE 4.2.

HOW LOW-BUT-RISING SCORES CAN LOWER AVERAGES.

500	510
500	510
500	510
500	510
500	510
500	510
500	510
500	430
500	430
400	430
Mean 490	Mean 486

In the left column, assume all 500s are SAT scores for white students and the 400 is the SAT score for minority students. The average of all scores is 490.

In the right column, assume all 510s are SAT scores for white students and all 430s are SAT scores for minorities. Minority scores have been rising faster than scores for white students. However, in the column on the left, minority students account for only 10 percent of the scores, whereas on the right, they account for 30 percent. Thus, all subgroup scores have risen, but the overall average has declined. This is the kind of "decline" that occurs when a group with low-but-improving scores accounts for a larger and larger proportion of the total scores. Since about 1970, minority test-takers have increased from 10 percent of the total to 30 percent.

it turned out: the writing and reading I did as part of my job stood me in good stead. On the other hand, if I had not read a couple of booklets on the SAT math, I likely would have been well below average. A number of questions on the SAT-M look impossible to solve until one remembers a simple process learned in 8th or 9th grade: how to factor an equation. I had not factored an equation for 24 years. If I had not boned up using some SAT practice booklets, I would not have recognized that a lot of complicated-looking questions had simple, quick solutions if one only remembered how to factor an equation.

SAT-V scores, however, might well decline. As an explanation of why this may be so, I offer the following example of a group of students I studied in Rhode Island who were taking part in a project concerning the search for the *Titanic*. As part of their project they read books, watched movies about submarines and life under the sea, and organized themselves into teams to play computer simulation games about the search. Because they were in Rhode Island, they were able to go to the nearby Woods Hole Oceanographic Institute and interview and videotape Robert Ballard, the man who led the actual successful search for the *Titanic*. At the end of the project, they constructed a multimedia display to show the rest of the school what they had been up to. It seemed to me that the project was both rich and rigorous. However, in terms of getting their SAT-V scores up, the students would have been advised to spend the same amount of time reading material that might increase their vocabulary.

Finally, as noted in the beginning, whether or not people believe that SAT scores have "plummeted" or "plunged" depends a great deal on how the data are displayed. Figure 4.3 shows the "Great SAT Decline" as graphed in the periodical *Public Interest* by Murray and Herrnstein (1992). Note that they used a 100-point scale, from 400 to 500. Also, *Public Interest* is a small-format magazine, so the time-frame scale is somewhat compressed by space constraints.

Consider now Figure 4.4. This graph is taken from "Perspectives on Education in America," more popularly known as "The Sandia Report" (Carson, Huelskamp, and Woodall 1993). The Sandia engineers sought to display SAT test score trends not only for the individual tests but for the total score, or, as they called it, the "combined" score. Thus they were require to use a 600-point scale running from 400 to 1000. They also used eight-and-a-half-by-eleven-inch paper for their report, so their time frame is more expanded than that used in the *Public Interest* graph. The bottom two curves of Figure 4.4 present precisely the same data as are presented by Murray and Herrnstein in Figure 4.3.

A comparison of these curves indicates that whereas a picture might be worth a thousand words, it can also create an image that might mislead. Looking at the Murray-Herrnstein graph, people might well be inclined to cluck their tongues and worry. The Sandia graph looks much less dire.

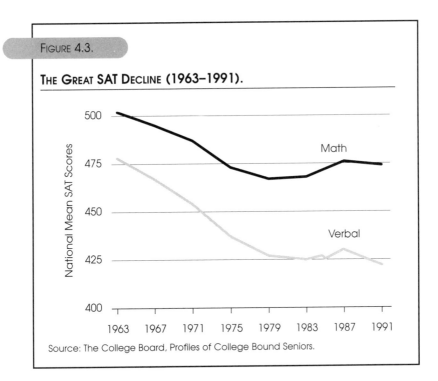

FIGURE 4.3.

THE GREAT SAT DECLINE (1963–1991).

Source: The College Board, Profiles of College Bound Seniors.

Whatever one thinks of the practical implications of the SAT decline, it is clear that the decline has been used as a battering ram by those who wish, for one reason or another, to criticize U.S. schools. The Wirtz panel's report was a model of thoroughness, sifting through the maze of data, analyzing parallel trends in other indicators, testing various hypotheses with sophisticated statistical tests and models. Later reports, however, were reduced to the simplicity of a sound bite. For instance, in its list of why and how we are *A Nation at Risk,* the authors of that document wrote, simply and simplistically, "The College Board's Scholastic Aptitude Tests (SAT) demonstrate a virtually unbroken decline from 1963 to 1980. Average verbal scores fell over 50 points and average mathematics scores dropped nearly 40 points" (National Commission on Excellence in Education, April 1983, p. 9). All subtlety is lost; all indications of why the decline occurred are missing.

One final issue surrounding the SAT requires some discussion: the issue of "recentering." Every five years or so, the publishers of

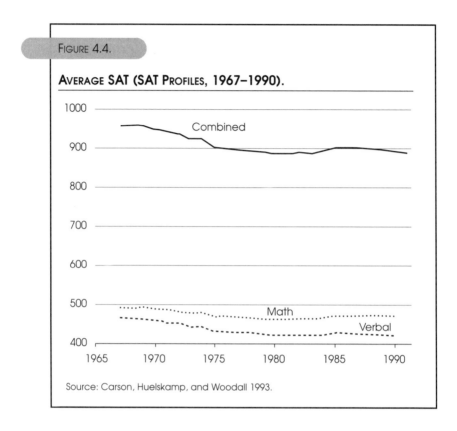

FIGURE 4.4.

AVERAGE SAT (SAT PROFILES, 1967–1990).

Source: Carson, Huelskamp, and Woodall 1993.

commercial achievement tests "renorm" the test. The norm in these tests is the average score—the 50th percentile—and the raw score that corresponds to that norm might (does) change from time to time. On one vocabulary test, say, the average score might be 19 out of 40 correct at one time and 22 out of 40 correct five years later. The norm has changed. Renormings adjust for these changes. Test companies renorm their tests about every five years, and no one thinks twice about it.

Until 1995, however, the SAT had never been renormed. The 10,654 white kids living in the Northeast and aiming for Ivy League and Seven Sisters colleges set the standards in 1941, and those standards remained fixed for more than 50 years. Using a straightforward statistical scaling technique, the College Board assigned the average score of these elite kids to be the scaled score of 500. That was fine for many years because, although these Ivy League–bound kids were an elite compared with the nation as a whole, they *were* pretty typical of the students who were taking the SAT. But this is no longer true. As noted, 43 percent of all seniors around the nation—more than a million students each year—take the SAT. Minority kids now make up 30 percent of the pool, and lots of SAT-takers come from low-income families. Whereas 40 percent of the standard-setters went to college prep high schools, 88 of those who take the SAT today are in public schools.

So, the College Board reasoned, although the old norms were fine for the 1941 elite, the sample has changed radically. In the beginning, 500 represented the average score for those students who were elite overall *and* typical of those taking the SAT. But that is no longer true. So, the board reasoned further, let us renorm the test so that 500 once again represents the score of the typical test-taker. The board called this renorming a "recentering," and this very common procedure unleashed a torrent of protest.

"You are trying to hide the fact that achievement is down," yelled the critics. "You're trying to make kids look good." And so forth. There really is no substance behind these criticisms, although they fit the tenor of the day. The College Board has been careful to provide information that links the new scale to the old, and this information is needed: without that link we couldn't track changes over time. But since the link is there, these longitudinal comparisons can be, and no doubt will be, made.

To repeat, given the extraordinary demographic changes in the students taking the SAT, the College Board decided that 500 no longer represented the score of the typical student and acted to make it represent what it did when the SAT took its modern form in 1941. It's that simple.

In Sum

When someone says, "SAT scores have plummeted," you can respond, "Not if you take into account demographic changes in the students who take the SAT." When the standards on the SAT were set and the average score was 500, that score was attained by an affluent group of white high school students living in the Northeast. Almost half had attended private college-prep high schools. Currently, 88 percent of the test-takers attend public school, more than half are female, nearly a third are minority, and nearly a third report family incomes under $30,000 a year. When the standards were set, the SAT was taken by only 10,654 students. In 1995, 1,067,000 seniors, or 43 percent of the entire national senior class, took the test—a much deeper dig into the talent pool.

All of these changes are associated with lower test scores. In fact, the decline began as colleges opened their doors to more women and to minorities. The scores of minorities have been rising for 20 years now, but because they are below the scores of white students and because minorities have accounted for more and more of the test-taking sample, they have had the apparent effect of depressing the overall average. But a "decline" that comes from adding in more lower scores from groups starting to take the test is very different from a decline that affects all groups.

If the standard-setting group is compared with a demographically similar group today, the mathematics scores show no decline and the verbal scores show only a small (22-point) decline. This means that on the verbal test, the students are getting wrong about 3 more of the 85 questions than were the standard-setters. Given the massive changes in how people process information—television viewing, videogames, and so forth, this decline hardly portends a crisis or warrants the word "plummet."

You can also point out that the SAT was designed only to supplement the rest of the high school record and that both its sponsor, the College Board, and its developer, Educational Testing Service, have long argued that it is not a measure of school quality or school outcomes.

References

Bracey, G.W. (May 1989). "The $150 Dollar Redundancy." *Phi Delta Kappan* 70, 9:698–702.

Bracey, G.W. (November 21, 1990)."SAT's: Miserable or Miraculous?" *Education Week,* p. 44.

Brigham, C.C., et al. (1926). "The Scholastic Aptitude Test of the College Entrance Examination Board." In *The Work of the College Entrance Examination Board, 1901–1925,* edited by T.S. Fiske. New York: Ginn and Company. Cited in *The College Board Admissions Testing Program,* edited by W.H. Argoff (New York, College Board, 1971), p. 2.

Carson, C.C., R.M. Huelskamp, and T.D. Woodall. (May/June 1993). "Perspectives on Education in America." *Journal of Educational Research,* 86, 5: 261–310.

The College Board. (1977). "On Further Examination." New York: Author.

Crouse, J., and D. Trusheim. (1988). *The Case Against the SAT.* Chicago: University of Chicago Press.

Murray, C., and R. Herrnstein. (Winter 1992). "What's Really Behind the SAT-Score Decline?" *The Public Interest* 106: 26–32.

National Commission on Excellence in Education. (April 1983). *A Nation at Risk: A Report to the Nation.* Washington, D.C.: U.S. Government Printing Office.

The Shrinking SAT Elite

What do I say when someone says, "The proportion of students scoring very high on the SAT has plummeted"?

This is often said by those who wish to argue that not only have *average* scores fallen, but, even worse, our nation's most able students are not what they used to be. This view is so widespread that it afflicted even a publication that should have known better, *Education Week,* and caused that publication's editors to make a major error, an error corrected in the following discussion. This contention is also often linked with another: that our best are far behind the best of other nations (the latter argument is rebutted in Chapter 7, which deals with international comparisons). An important point to remember is that the proportion of high-scoring students cited developed under the old SAT scale—that is, before the "recentering" described at the end of the previous chapter.

In Brief

In brief, you can say the following:

• The proportion of students scoring high on the SAT-V is smaller than it used to be, but the word "plummet" is a vast overstatement of the change.

• The proportion of students scoring well on the SAT-M has been rising in the last 15 years and is at an all-time high, a result that cannot be accounted for by high-scoring Asian students. Asian students do score higher on the SAT math section than do other ethnic groups, but they are far too few in number to account for the growth seen.

In Detail

The earliest data on high-scoring students, as reported in a background paper for *On Further Examination,* is from 1966–67 (Jackson 1976). These scores are grouped by 100-point intervals, so the comparisons cannot be too refined. Nonetheless, we can say that in 1966 (the third year of the SAT's long decline), 2.3 percent of the students scored above 700 on the SAT-V, and in 1995, 1.2 percent had such high scores. We also know from the statistical properties of the normal curve that 2.3 percent of the standard-setting elite in 1941 scored above 700 (more later on how we know this). Thus, the proportion of these super-high scorers has been roughly halved. However, 1966 appears to have been a high point. By 1968 the proportion was at 1.8 and by 1972, 1.1. The proportion appears to have stabilized at either 1.1 or 1.2 ever since 1972, that is, for 25 years.

The trend line for high-scorers on the SAT-V presents a most curious curve, shown in Figure 5.1. The curve is stable at 2.3 percent from the test's inception until 1966, then falls for six years and is stable from 1972 to the present. Whether or not a change from 2.3 percent to 1.1 percent can be called a "plunge," such a curve does not seem to fit with an assertion that things have been getting worse for a long time. Nor does it seem likely that such a rapid decline would be caused by some problem that suddenly appeared in the school system.

The picture for students scoring above 700 on the SAT-M appears quite different from that for the SAT-V. In 1966, 3.9 percent of all students scored above 700. By 1975, this proportion had fallen to 3.1 percent. By 1995, the proportion had risen to 5.6 percent—an all-time high. Thus, the highest scorers on the SAT-M are not only *not* plummeting out of sight, they are growing in number and proportion. (It is more important to talk about SAT scores in terms of pro-

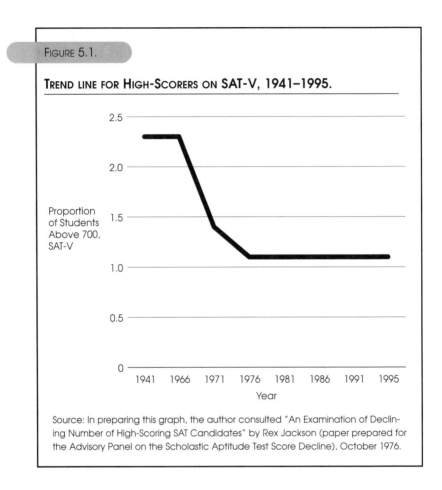

FIGURE 5.1.

TREND LINE FOR HIGH-SCORERS ON SAT-V, 1941–1995.

Source: In preparing this graph, the author consulted "An Examination of Declining Number of High-Scoring SAT Candidates" by Rex Jackson (paper prepared for the Advisory Panel on the Scholastic Aptitude Test Score Decline), October 1976.

portion than in terms of number. With the passing of the baby boom, the number of high school seniors declined virtually every year from 1977 to 1994. This would lead us to expect smaller *numbers* of students with high scores. The *proportion* of students scoring at a given level, however, is independent of the number taking the test.) As with the SAT-V, 2.3 percent of the elite standard-setting group in 1941 scored above 700. The current proportion is thus well over twice as large as the proportion of the 1941 elite.

If we change our definition of "high scorers" to include those scoring over 600, we see a somewhat different picture. In 1966, 12.5 percent of all students scored above 600 on the SAT-V. This would compare with 15 percent of the 1941 standard setters. By 1975 this figure had fallen to 7.6 percent. This does appear to be a sizable decline in high scorers. In 1995 the proportion was 8.3 percent, a slight increase but not a whopping gain. It thus appears, however, that the proportion of high-scoring students on the verbal section has, at worst, remained stable over the last 20 years. The proportion is not plummeting.

In 1966, 17.9 percent of the students scored 600 or better on the SAT-M. By 1975 this proportion had fallen to 15.1 percent, which is almost identical to the 15 percent of the standard-setting group of 1941. In 1995 fully 21.5 percent of the students got at least 600! Thus, the SAT-M shows a very different picture than the SAT-V: a small decline followed by a recovery of significant proportions. In fact, the proportion of students scoring above 600 on the SAT-M is at an *all-time high*. Please note again that all of these calculations use the old SAT scale, not the recentered one (as do all subsequent scores as well).

What accounts for the difference between the verbal trend and the math trend? No direct answer is obvious, but several factors suggest themselves. One is television. David Berliner, coauthor of *The Manufactured Crisis* (1995), contends that starting in the early 1960s our major form of recreation changed and we spent more and more time in front of the tube. This is plausible. It is also the case that over the last 15 years, an increasing number of students who do not speak English as their native language have taken the SAT. That the proportion of students scoring well on the SAT-V has remained stable under these conditions is somewhat surprising and hardly a cause for despair.

In the education chapter of *The Candidate's Handbook, 1996,* a publication of the conservative Heritage Foundation, Denis Doyle asserts that the mathematics trend is due to Asian immigrants and Asian American students. This is a common assertion, and it is totally false. It is true that Asian students score much higher than other ethnic groups on the SAT-M, garnering an average score in 1995 of 538 compared with the national average of 482. But they are too few in number to account for the changes seen. In 1982 Asian students accounted for 4 percent of the test-taking group and in 1995, 8 percent. Even if *all* of the new Asian students scored above 600, which they don't, this 4 percentage-point increase in Asian students would not account for the increase in high scorers. Furthermore, if we remove the Asian students from the sample, we find that in 1982, 6.5 percent of the students scored above 650, while in 1995 10.5 percent attained such scores. Thus we have tremendous growth in high scores even without including Asian Americans.

A much more likely cause for the increase is the change in the kinds of mathematics courses American students have taken over the last 15 years. In 1982 only 24 percent of students took both algebra II and plane geometry; by 1992 that figure had increased to 50 percent. Similar increases are seen for more advanced mathematics courses and for all sciences. If these increases did nothing more than keep the earlier learned skills current, they likely would cause some increase in the SAT-M.

The preceding analysis of SAT trends includes a lot of technical information, so let's summarize: The proportion of high scorers on the SAT-V did fall; it is about half of what it once was, and that proportion has been stable for about 25 years. The proportion of students scoring high on the SAT-M showed a much smaller decline; over the last 15 years it has been rising and currently rests at an all-time high.

And what of *Education Week*'s error? It is instructive to examine it, for it reveals a very common tendency of observers when looking at education data. Like many, the editors of *Education Week* assumed the worst. In February 1993, the paper began a multipart look at what had happened since the appearance of *A Nation at Risk,* which would celebrate its 10th anniversary in April 1993. In the opening essay, the editors asked, in general, what had happened since *Risk's* publication, and their answer was, in general, "not much." They reported that the "proportion of high school students performing at high levels remains infinitesimally small. For instance, in the last decade the number and proportion of students scoring above 650 on the SAT verbal and mathematics has declined." In a box in the margins, *Education Week* presented the numbers shown in Figure 5.2.

The statistics in Figure 5.2 certainly do make it appear that both the number and proportion of high scorers are falling. A check of the College Board's "Profiles of College Bound Seniors" for the years in question, however, revealed a problem. The numbers for 1982 are

---

FIGURE 5.2.

NUMBER (AND PROPORTION) OF STUDENTS SCORING ABOVE 650 ON THE SAT VERBAL AND MATHEMATICS, ACCORDING TO EDUCATION WEEK.

	1982	1992
Verbal	29,921 (3)	22,754 (2)
Mathematics	70,352 (7)	58,662 (6)

Source: *Education Week,* February 10, 1993.

---

correct; the numbers for 1992 are correct as far as they go—but they don't go far enough. The "Profiles" group students by 40-point intervals. Thus, when looking at the table, one sees all of the students who scored between 200 and 240 on one line, then all of those who scored between 250 and 290 on another line, and so forth. The numbers that *Education Week* used for 1992 are only for the group scoring between 650 and 690, thereby omitting all students who scored above 700. When these are added, the picture looks quite different, as shown in Figure 5.3.

Thus, contrary to the editors' assertion of a decline, we find a stable proportion for the verbal test and a rising proportion for mathe-

---

FIGURE 5.3.

NUMBER (AND PROPORTION) OF STUDENTS ACTUALLY SCORING ABOVE 650 ON THE SAT VERBAL AND MATHEMATICS.

	1982	1992	1995
Verbal	29,921 (3)	32,903 (3)	39,003 (4)
Mathematics	70,352 (7)	104,401 (10)	132,848 (12)

---

matics. I requested that the paper print a front-page correction. They did not, although they published my letter noting the error. At the end of my letter, they appended an editorial note saying that it was still a tiny proportion. This led me to write a second letter observing that the SAT's developers had imposed a bell curve on the initial data, and that it was in the nature of bell curves that not many people score very high (or very low). I noted that although 10 percent of the students in 1992 scored above 650 on the SAT-M, only 6.68 percent of the standard-setting elite had attained this lofty status. The proportion scoring above 650 has since risen to 12 percent, an all-time high (the 12 percent is calculated with the old SAT scale, not the "recentered" one of recent vintage).

In Sum

When someone says, "The proportion of students scoring very high on the SAT has plummeted," you can respond, "It depends on which test you look at. The proportion of students scoring high on the verbal test has fallen somewhat, but the proportion of students doing well on the math test is at an all-time high. This cannot be accounted for by the high scores of Asian American students."

The proportion of students scoring above 650 on the SAT verbal is about half of what it was in 1941, when the standards were set. Some of this is no doubt due to television. Some of it is due to the increasing number of students who do not speak English as a native language. And some of it is due to other factors, including easier-to-read textbooks.

The proportion of students scoring above 650 on the SAT math test is at a record high and has been growing over the last decade. Whereas Asian students score higher than any other ethnic group, they are far too few in number to account for much of the growth. Between 1981 and 1995, the proportion of Asian American students taking the test doubled, but that meant only that they now constitute 8 percent of those taking the test instead of 4 percent. And when Asian students are removed from the sample, we find that in 1982, 6.8 percent of the students scored above 650, whereas in 1995 10.7 percent attained such scores—an impressive increase in high scorers. Looking at all test-takers, we see a 75 percent gain in the proportion of students scoring above 650; with Asian students removed from the sample, there is still a 57 percent gain.

The growth in the percentage of high-scoring students probably comes from changes in course-taking patterns. Since the late 1960s and especially since 1982, a higher and higher proportion of students has been taking more and more math and science courses. Course-taking patterns in English have been much less influenced by changes in requirements; most states already required three or four years of English when states began increasing requirements in the 1980s. Nevertheless, the proportion of students scoring above 650 on the SAT verbal has risen from 3.0 percent in 1982 to 3.9 percent in 1995.

References

Berliner, D., and B.J. Biddle. (1995). *The Manufactured Crisis: Myths, Fraud, and the Attack on America's Public Schools*. Reading, Mass.: Addison-Wesley Publishing Company.

Education Week. (February 10, 1993). "From Risk to Renewal." Special Report, p. 4.

The Heritage Foundation. (1996). *The Candidate's Handbook, 1996*. Washington, D.C.: Author.

Jackson, R. (October 1976). "An Examination of Declining Numbers of High-Scoring SAT Candidates." Paper prepared for the Advisory Panel of the Scholastic Aptitude Test Score Decline. New York: College Entrance Examination Board.

Knowledge Nostalgia

What do I say when someone says, "Kids don't know as much as they used to"?

This notion comes from the widespread stories reporting that U.S. students cannot find Mexico on a map and don't know who important historical figures were. Former Assistant Secretary of Education Chester E. Finn Jr. begins his book *We Must Take Charge* (1991) with a sad tale of ignoramuses sharing his flight from Minneapolis to Frankfurt. They don't know whether they gain or lose time en route, and one says it's the first time he's ever flown over the Pacific. Finn and fellow conservative Diane Ravitch contributed heavily to the notion that U.S. kids today are more ignorant than previous generations through the publication of their book on students' knowledge of history and literature, *What Do Our 17-Year-Olds Know?* (1987). Their answer was, essentially, "not much": "If there were such a thing as a national report card for those studying American history and literature, then we would have to say that this nationally representative sample of 11th-grade students earns failing marks in both subjects" (p.1). E.D. Hirsch's various works on "cultural literacy" (1987), while not polemics like Ravitch and Finn's, also contribute to the implication that such literacy is gravely lacking.

The impression of declining knowledge is also created by the media's selective reporting. In February 1992 the Second International Assessment of Educational Progress in Mathematics and Science was released (Lapointe, Mead, and Askew 1992; Lapointe, Askew, and Mead 1992). Ranks for the United States were, by and large, low (although U.S. *scores* were quite close to the international average). The study received wide coverage in both print and electronic media. "An 'F' in World Competition" was how *Newsweek* headlined the story. In July 1992, *How in the World Do Students Read?* appeared (Elley 1992). Not one media outlet reported on this study of reading skills in 31 nations, in which U.S. students finished second. Similarly, in the fall of 1995, a generally upbeat assessment of geography appeared, and little coverage ensued. When a less optimistic history assessment came out a few weeks later, it was page-one news in the *Washington Post,* where education writer Rene Sanchez called it a "dismal report card" in his opening paragraph (1995). Leaving his own publication, *Harper's* editor Lewis Lapham took to the op-ed page of the *New York Times* to call the results "a coroner's report" for democracy (1995).

In Brief

In brief, you can say the following:

- The bulk of the evidence shows that U.S. students today read better than ever, know more mathematics and science, and know at least as much about literature and history as their parents and grandparents did, and probably more.
- You can remind the skeptic that most of what he or she knows has probably been learned in the many years since leaving school. You can also remind people that those who find something easy to accomplish too often do not understand that the same accomplishment can be difficult for others. The people who have evaluated what school children know and can do are the people who find book learning the easiest thing in the world to do.
- You can accuse the speakers of nostalgia mongering.

In Detail

The evidence indicates, rather strongly, that students read at least as well as they used to, know more math and science than ever, and know at least as much about history and geography as in past years. In terms of history, consider this:

> A large majority of the students showed that they had virtually no knowledge of elementary aspects of American history. They could not identify such names as Abraham Lincoln, Thomas Jefferson, Andrew Jackson, or Theodore Roosevelt. . . . Most of our students do not have the faintest notion of what this country looks like. St. Louis was placed on the Pacific Ocean, Lake Huron, Lake Erie, the Atlantic Ocean, Ohio River, St. Lawrence River, and almost every place else.

This incensed prose could readily have come from Ravitch and Finn or in reaction to the 1995 history assessment. In fact, it comes from a story in the *New York Times* about its own survey of students. The *Times* was so outraged, it put the story on page one, right next to its other major headline of the day: "Patton Attacks East of El Guettar." April 4, 1943. Given the task of identifying famous Americans' professions, students claimed that Walt Whitman was a missionary to the Far East, a pioneer, a colonizer, an explorer, a speculator, an unpatriotic writer, a humorist, a musician, a composer, and a columnist. "Hundreds of students listed Whitman as being an orchestra leader." Because the *Times* made no further comment on this, we can assume that the editors did not make the connection to Paul Whiteman, a popular bandleader of the time.

What particularly galled the *Times* was that these ignoramuses were not high school students, they were college freshmen. The *Times* did not take note of the fact, but we can, that in 1943, the high school graduation rate was about 45 percent. Of these, about 15 percent went on to college. So these ignoramuses were an elite group of ignoramuses—the upper 7 percent of the student body. It is worth noting that the *Times* did not blame the public schools for the students' poor performance; such laying of blame would begin shortly after World War II. Rather, the *Times* appears to have assumed that the students forgot information that they once had known.

In 1957, with Cold War tensions high, journalist Harrison Salisbury undertook a survey for *McCall's* to find out how much Americans knew about the Soviet Union. In the June issue, Salisbury reported that only 71 percent of American *college graduates* could name the capital of the Soviet empire; only 21 percent could name a single Russian author; and only 24 percent could name a single Russian composer. Apparently, most college grads became alumni without ever encountering Tolstoy or Dostoyevsky or Tchaikovsky or Rimsky-Korsakov. If they knew who wrote *War and Peace* or *Crime and Punishment,* they didn't let on.

Yet, in his 1970 tome, *Crisis in the Classroom,* Charles Silberman cited a study by Educational Testing Service, which had looked at 186 comparisons of students' knowledge at different points in time. All had been conducted since World War II. One hundred and seventy-six of them favored the more recent time.[1] (One might wonder, then, where the "crisis" in the classroom lay. For Silberman it lay in the comparison of what schools were with what they could be. He had visited a number of English informal "infant schools" at the early elementary grade level and been greatly impressed with their humanity and the way children were treated. In comparison with these classrooms, American schools were "grim, repressive, joyless" p. 116.)

To say that students were ignorant then and things worked out OK is not to say it's all right to be ignorant now. This is not the Forrest Gump defense of schooling. But Americans (and maybe people in other nations) have an overwhelming tendency to think there was a Golden Age of education, a state of grace from which we have fallen and to which we must struggle to return. In his book *The Thirteenth Man* (1988), the late Terrel Bell, secretary of education in the Reagan administration, wrote,

> If we are frank with ourselves, we must acknowledge that for most Americans, neither diligence in learning nor rigorous standards of performance prevail. . . . How do we once again become a nation of learners, in which attitudes toward intellectual pursuit and quality of work have excellence as their core? (p. 167)

---

[1] The study Silberman refers to was published in *Toward a Social Report.* (1969). Washington, D.C.: Department of Health, Education, and Welfare.

This is a typical nostalgic yearning, and I am sorry I didn't write Bell before he died to say, "Ted, we have never been a nation of learners, and to get some idea of why, take a look at the inscription on the Statue of Liberty. It does not say 'Send me your 1250 SATs, your college grads yearning to learn.' It says 'Send me your tired, your poor, your huddled masses yearning to be free. . . .' What we have accomplished with those huddled masses is stunning. And if the trends on test scores are to be believed, we are closer now than at any time in the past to being a 'nation of learners.' "

In terms of history, only one study exists that actually inquired how much people knew in the past. It is, however, among the most carefully constructed and conducted in educational research, and it corroborates inferences that we might make from the *New York Times* and *McCall's* surveys. Dale Whittington of Cleveland State University gathered questions and results from a variety of assessments carried out in the past—1917, 1933, 1944, and 1964—and compared the results with those of Finn and Ravitch. Her conclusion:

> Each group [of test-takers] performed about the same on the particular set of test questions designed for them to take. . . . Comparisons of student performance on test questions that matched the content of specific questions in the test used by Ravitch and Finn seem to confirm the results of this study that, for the most part, students of the 1980s are not demonstrably different from students of their parents' or grandparents' generation in terms of their knowledge of American history.
>
> One major implication of the results of this study is that the perception of a decline in the "results" of American education is open to question. Indeed, given the reduced dropout rate and less elitist composition of the 17-year-old student body today, one could argue that students today know more American history than did their peers of the past (Whittington 1992, p. 787).

Whittington probably should have made more of this conclusion, because the "elitist composition" of secondary schools becomes quite extreme quite rapidly in her study. In 1987, 83 percent of U.S. students graduated from high school on time. In 1964, the rate was around 70 percent; in 1944, about 45 percent; in 1933, about 30 percent; and in 1917, about 15 percent. That the overwhelming majority of teenagers today know what only an elite were exposed to 50 or more years ago is quite remarkable.

Ravitch and Finn also guaranteed that they would get "miserable" results, although they appear not to have been aware of the statistical technicality that ensured this outcome. They claimed that they were administering a criterion-referenced test. However, the items provided to them by Educational Testing Service had the prime statistical property of most norm-referenced items: on average, 50 percent of the students got the item wrong. (Norm-referenced testmakers favor items with a 50 percent average failure rate because such a pass-fail rate will maximally spread out the test scores—a prime goal of a norm-referenced test.) Thus, when Ravitch and Finn later set their passing score at 60 percent, they guaranteed a high failure rate.

When it comes to reading, many studies offer results similar to those Whittington found for history. The field of reading has produced many "then-and-now" studies, with "then" and "now" being defined by different years depending on when the study was done. For instance, Leo Fay and Roger Farr at Indiana University administered the 1946 Iowa Tests of Basic Skills to students in Indiana in 1974. They then compared these students' results with what was obtained in 1946. In this study, "then" was defined as 1946, "now" as 1974. By and large, the students in 1974 outperformed those in 1946 (Kaestle, Damon-Moore, Stedman, Tinsley, and Trollinger 1991).

However, such studies are fraught with design and interpretive difficulties. Indiana in 1974 was a far different state than in 1946. It was, like other states, permeated with television. It was far more urbanized and less rural than it had been 28 years earlier. And it was more ethnically diverse. Still, in a review of then-and-now studies spanning a hundred years, Carl Kaestle and his colleagues concluded that "school children of the same age and socioeconomic status have been performing at similar levels [of reading] throughout most of the twentieth century" (1991, p. 89).

Actually, this analysis vastly understates the gains in reading. As we saw in connection with the Whittington history study, progressing through the 20th century, we find a higher and higher percentage of students of lower socioeconomic status attending school. Students of high socioeconomic status might be reading today at the same levels as "throughout most of the twentieth century," but for about half of that century, children of the poor were hardly reading at all.

There is a myth, usually invoked against bilingual education programs, that immigrants arriving on these shores in the early part of this century were thrown into a "sink or swim" situation, and that most of them fared OK in school despite not speaking English. No, they didn't. Most of them sank. Like stones. They simply weren't noticed because so many native-born children also were not attending school, and the immigrants just melted into this larger crowd.

In math and science, no studies have documented long-term trends. Moreover, these fields have undergone vast changes in teaching methods. The New Math of the 1960s may have flopped badly, but it started people thinking afresh about how to teach math. The New Physics of the same era might also have had many flaws, but it moved us out of the 19th-century focus on Newton's laws of motion into the 20th-century study of particle physics. The New Biology, by all accounts, was successful in moving us away from courses in which students did little more than memorize the characteristics of phyla.

In the short term, the decade from 1982 to 1992 saw a dramatic increase in the number of students taking more advanced courses in mathematics and the various sciences. Diane Ravitch once commented that this meant that schools were now teaching in three years what used to require only two. A study conducted by the University of Wisconsin under the aegis of the Council of Chief State School Officers, however, concluded that there had been no loss of quality, rigor, or content because of the expansion of course-taking (1994).

Finally, we need to take note of the human foible mentioned at the beginning of this chapter: a person who finds something easy to accomplish often doesn't realize how hard that something can be for someone else. At one point in my life, I was writing a magazine article a month and two newspaper articles a week. My wife was flabbergasted at how I could find fresh things to say and get them down clearly on paper. She generally writes nothing more complicated than her name. But this same wife who is awed by writing has on numerous occasions heard a piece of classical music for the first time and, before it was finished, worked out a ballet routine to it. I have two left feet and couldn't choreograph one minute of music.

People who work in universities are (1) the people who are most capable of succeeding at academic work and (2) the people who conduct most of the evaluations of schools. Almost all of the 43 papers commissioned for *A Nation at Risk* were written by academics. We can imagine them looking at, for example, NAEP mathematics results and being dumbfounded that the performance is no higher. Clearly, it must seem to them, the students aren't trying or they're not being taught well. In fact, both of those conclusions might be wrong. Still, as Daniel Tanner (1993) of Rutgers has pointed out, academics have never been supportive of K–12 education, whatever the reasons might be.

In Sum

When someone says, "Kids just don't know as much as they used to," you can say, "Yes, they do. They probably know more." The one study focusing on history found that kids today know at least as much as their parents' and grandparents' generations. Because more students would have dropped out in those earlier generations, the current generation of kids probably knows more. Numerous studies of reading skills indicate that kids read better now than they did earlier. And in terms of mathematics and science, students are taking courses in high school that were not available earlier. In science in particular, they are learning things that weren't even known in earlier times.

One book reported that of 186 comparisons of students at different points in time since World War II, 176 favored the students of more recent time. These studies likely underestimated the achievement of later kids. Shortly after World War II, the high school graduation rate passed the 50 percent mark and continued to increase into the 1980s. Thus, because more kids were staying in school, each newer study was testing a more complete, less elite sample of the population.

You can remind your commentator that nostalgia about what earlier generations knew is very prevalent, has been for quite a while—and is wrong. You can also note that adults tend to have unrealistic expectations for the younger generation. Both of these attributes of adults were displayed in a lyric from the 1960 musical *Bye Bye Birdie*: "Why can't they be like we were, perfect in every way? Oh, what's the matter with kids today?"

References

Bell, T. (1988). *The Thirteenth Man*. New York: Free Press.

Council of Chief State School Officers. (1994). *State Indicators in Mathematics and Science Education 1993*. Washington, D.C.: Author.

Elley, W.B. (July 1992). *How in the World Do Students Read? IEA Study of Reading Literacy*. Netherlands: International Association for the Evaluation of Educational Achievement. ED360613. Available from ERIC Document Reproduction Service, 1-800-443-3742.

Finn, C.E. Jr. (1991). *We Must Take Charge*. New York: Free Press.

Hirsch, E.D. Jr. (1987). *Cultural Literacy*. Boston: Houghton Mifflin.

Kaestle, C., H. Damon-Moore, L. Stedman, K. Tinsley, and W. Trollinger Jr. (1991). *Literacy in the United States: Readers and Reading Since 1880*. New Haven, Conn: Yale University Press.

Lapham, L. (Dec. 2, 1995). "Ignorance Passes the Point of No Return." *The New York Times*, p. A-21.

Lapointe, A.E., N.A. Mead, and J.M. Askew. (1992). *Learning Mathematics*. Princeton, N.J.: Educational Testing Service.

Lapointe, A.E., J.M. Askew, and N.A. Mead. (1992). *Learning Science*. Princeton, N.J.: Educational Testing Service.

Ravitch, D., and C.E. Finn Jr. (1987). *What Do Our 17-Year-Olds Know?* New York: Harper and Row.

Sanchez, Rene. (Nov. 2, 1995). "Knowing the Past May Be History, U.S. Test Reveals." *The Washington Post*, p. A-1.

Silberman, C. (1970). *Crisis in the Classroom*. New York: Random House.

Tanner, Daniel. (December 1993). "A Nation 'Truly' at Risk." *Phi Delta Kappan* 75,4: 288–297.

Whittington, D. (Winter 1988). "What Have 17-Year-Olds Known in the Past?" *American Educational Research Journal* 25,4: 759–780.

International Comparisons

What do I say when someone says, "It doesn't matter if kids know more today than they did 20 years ago; what matters is what they know compared with what German and Japanese kids know, and in those comparisons, they don't know much"?

Variations of this statement are among the most common declarations made by the school bashers. Improvements in domestic indicators of achievement are irrelevant. Albert Shanker, president of the American Federation of Teachers, in reaction to a *USA Today* article about my work (Kelly 1991) said, "I don't care if my 1990 car drives a little better than my 1970 car. I care if it drives as well as those German and Japanese models parked across the street." Many people feel as Shanker does, meaning, for one thing, that this chapter will be by far the longest of the book. It will also contain some of the most complicated analyses, which are, even so, not so hard to understand.

Shanker has mentioned international comparisons many times. He began one of his paid Sunday *New York Times* advertisement-columns this way: "The achievement of U.S. students in grades K–12 is very poor" (June 27, 1993). This was just a warm-up. The next week Shanker led off with, "American students are performing at much lower levels than students in other industrial nations" (July 4, 1993). Still not satisfied, Shanker returned for a third straight week and started his advertisement by saying, "International examinations designed to compare students from all over the world usually show American students at or near the bottom" (July 11, 1993). Shanker provided no data, and none of these statements is true.

Louis V. Gerstner, CEO of IBM, in a book written mostly by Denis Doyle but with Gerstner's name as the lead author, declared that "American high schoolers come in last or next to last in virtually every international measure" (1994, p. 5.) *Washington Post* pundit Charles Krauthammer made the next leap of hyperbole to declare that "we've gotten used to finishing dead last" in international comparisons (July 15, 1994).

The companion piece to these comments about the performance of the typical American student is the similar claim made about our best students. As voiced by C. Boyden Gray (former counsel to George Bush) and Evan J. Kemp (former chair of the Equal Employment Opportunity Commission), it comes out this way: "Yet even America's best high school students, as international comparisons reveal, rank far behind students in countries challenging us in the multinational marketplace" (Gray and Kemp 1993).

On January 31, 1996, the National Alliance of Business, the National Governors Association, the Business Roundtable, the American Federation of Teachers, and the U.S. Department of Education sponsored a full-page ad in the *New York Times* deploring the performance of American students in international comparisons. On the left-hand side of the page were 15 countries, listed by number. The United States was number 14, and the words "United States" were circled in bold strokes. To the right, the text read, "If this were a ranking in Olympic hockey, we would be outraged." The "Sixth Bracey Report on the Condition of Public Education" awarded all of these groups an Oscar for the most unethical ad of the year.

So, the belief that our students are shamed by those in other countries is widespread and much embedded. What can you say in response?

In Brief

In brief, you can say the following:

- People often confuse ranks and scores. In studies of mathematics and science, U.S. ranks are often low, but U.S. scores are near the international averages. In reading, U.S. ranks and average scores are both among the highest in the world. And the scores of our best students—those at the 90th, 95th, and 99th percentiles—*are* the world's best when compared with the scores of students from 31 other nations. In these comparisons, most of the countries are developed countries, and they score very close together. This means that a small difference in *score* will make a big difference in *rank*. The most recent reading study, for example, showed no statistically significant differences among countries all the way from the 2nd-place country through the 11th-place country.

- It often doesn't make sense to compare school systems the way they are compared in these studies. For instance, the most crucial event in a child's school career in Japan or Korea is whether or not he or she gets into college. Not many do. These children not only work hard in school, they go to school at night and on weekends, often at great expense to their parents. For American students, it is relatively easy to get into some college or university. Students with poor high school records can start at a community college and transfer later to a four-year institution if they want to and if their grades are good enough. So they don't work as hard in high school as perhaps they should. In college, the reverse holds. American students start to work hard, and many must also work at jobs. College is free in Japan, so staying on is not a burden to the family. Japanese college students go into virtual intellectual hibernation. They party, drink, carouse, and generally do everything but study. The course of their lives is already determined. Ken Schoolland, an American teaching at a college in Japan, reported in *Shogun's Ghosts: The Dark Side of Japanese Education* that students in his classes talked, lounged about, and cheated openly on tests (1990). He said he was instructed to award passing grades to anyone who showed up halfway regularly.

This is not to say that the Japanese system is inferior to ours. It is to say that it is important to compare entire systems, not just a couple of grades, as is usually done. It is also important to note the cultural baggage that is part and parcel of a school system. Schools do not exist in vacuums. The American version of childhood includes not just television but shopping malls, dating, and extracurricular activities. The Korean version of childhood includes this saying: "A high school student who sleeps four hours a night will get into college. A high school student who sleeps five hours a night will not."

In Detail

In terms of what you can learn from the numbers reported in international comparisons, keep in mind the enormous difference between a rank and a score, and always know which you're dealing with. As with the *New York Times* ad, most people talk in terms of ranks but act as though they're discussing performance. Ranks not only tell you nothing about performance, they *obscure* performance. *Scores* describe performance. If your child ranks at the 60th percentile on a test, you know your child did better than 60 percent of the other children taking the test, but you don't know anything about how well he or she did in absolute terms. Maybe all the kids were awful and yours was just better than 60 percent of a bunch of nincompoops.

A sports analogy is useful here. In the 1996 Summer Olympics in Atlanta, Michael Marsh ranked third of eight runners in his semifinal heat in the 200-meter dash. In the final, he finished dead last, eighth, even though he ran only .22 of a second slower than he had in the semifinal heat. Looking at the ranks for the finals, you can tell that Michael Johnson won, but not that he set a new world record. Nor could you tell that had Michael Marsh been able to improve his performance by 7 percent, he, not Michael Johnson, would have taken the gold—and set a world record better than Johnson's. In a list of ranks, someone *always* ranks last. Chances are that Michael Johnson does not call Michael Marsh "Pokey," even in jest.

Thus it is that American students sometimes (but not always) rank low in mathematics and science comparisons, but their scores

FIGURE 7.1.

U.S. RANKS AND SCORES ON IAEP-2, WITH INTERNATIONAL AVERAGES.

	Mathematics			Science		
Age	U.S. Rank*	U.S. Score	Int'l Average	U.S. Rank*	U.S Score	Int'l Average
9	9	58	64	3	65	63
13	14	55	63	13	67	70

*Ranks are based on 10 countries for 9-year-olds and 15 countries for 13-year-olds.

are near the international average. This is illustrated by the results of the Second International Assessment of Math and Science (IAEP-2) (Lapointe, Mead, and Askew 1992; Lapointe, Askew, and Mead 1992). Figure 7.1 presents the U.S. ranks and scores, along with the international averages.[1]

As noted, even where the ranks are low, the scores are not far from the international average. This is true even where the United States ranks high: U.S. 9-year-olds are ranked 3rd in science, but their average scores were only 2 points higher than those of their peers in other countries. If they had scored only 60 instead of their actual 65, they would have fallen to 8th place among the 10 countries. Similarly, U.S. 13-year-olds are ranked 13th of 15 nations even though their score is only 3 points below the international average. Had they managed to score 72, a mere 5 points more, they would have finished 5th.

---

[1] The international averages in this figure are higher than those calculated by Educational Testing Service for its reports on the study, *Learning Mathematics* and *Learning Science*. ETS simply added up the scores of all of the countries and divided by the number of countries. ETS included in this calculation countries with nonrepresentative populations. This would be a flaw under any circumstances, but in many instances, the scores of these nonrepresentative countries were quite low. The average, which I calculated for only those countries with representative samples, puts the United States in a worse light than does the ETS international average.

These results mean, in part, that most countries are tightly bunched together. It seems silly to make much ado about differences in ranks when the scores of the nations are so similar. It seems even sillier when we remember that virtually all of these scores come from 9- and 13-year-olds, students who are nowhere near completing their education.

But there is more to the data than just overall averages. We can learn a lot by looking at the variability and at the scores of sub-groups.

When I read tales of other countries' educational systems written by critics of our own, I get the impression that these nations have found the key to success for all students. Robert R. Spillane, long-time superintendent of one of the nation's largest and most respected school districts, Fairfax County, Virginia, once wrote, "Many countries are educating everybody to higher levels than we are" (*Education Week*, June 2, 1993, p. 36). Returning from Japan, former Assistant Secretary of Education Chester Finn said, "They [the Japanese] have shown that the average student can learn a whole lot more" (Richburg 1985). Comments like Spillane's and Finn's, however, turn out to be more fantasy than fact.

Consider Figure 7.2. This chart shows the IAEP-2 scores for 13-year-olds in mathematics (National Center for Education Statistics 1993). The average score is in the solid box in the middle of each bar.[2] The dark bars extend to the 25th percentile on the left and the 75th percentile on the right. The light bars then extend to the 5th and 95th percentiles.

What is striking about this graph is the huge variability of performance *within* each nation compared with the variability *among* nations. The scale on which these scores are plotted is the scale used in the United States for NAEP. Iowa and Mississippi are shown to

---

[2] Why, you might ask, is the average a box and not a point? It is because those who conduct these studies have adopted the convention of showing the average surrounded by something called a "confidence interval." A confidence interval is familiar to all of you, although you might not recognize it. When the results of a Gallup or Roper poll are reported, there is always a footnote saying something like, "This poll has a margin of error of plus or minus 4 percent." That is a confidence interval.

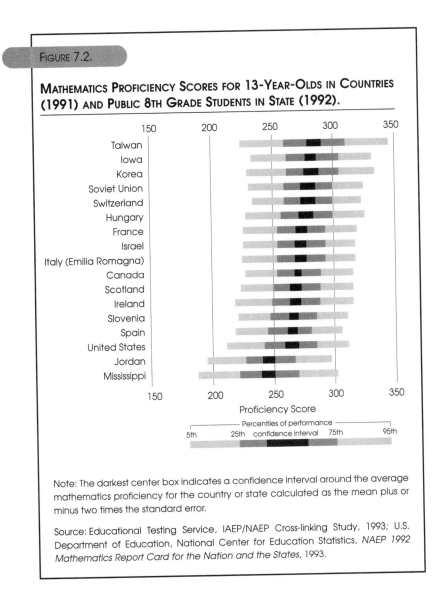

FIGURE 7.2.

MATHEMATICS PROFICIENCY SCORES FOR 13-YEAR-OLDS IN COUNTRIES (1991) AND PUBLIC 8TH GRADE STUDENTS IN STATE (1992).

Proficiency Score

Note: The darkest center box indicates a confidence interval around the average mathematics proficiency for the country or state calculated as the mean plus or minus two times the standard error.

Source: Educational Testing Service, IAEP/NAEP Cross-linking Study, 1993; U.S. Department of Education, National Center for Education Statistics, *NAEP 1992 Mathematics Report Card for the Nation and the States*, 1993.

indicate the range of state-level scores. The difference between the average proficiency scores for Jordan and Mississippi, tied at the bottom, and Iowa and Taiwan, at the top, is 39 NAEP scale points (which is .80 of a NAEP-scale standard deviation, by the way). On the other hand, the span between the 5th percentile and the 95th percentile scores for Taiwan covers 123 NAEP scale points. If the figure were extended to include the 1st and 99th percentiles, Taiwan's spread would be more than 150 points. This graph strongly suggests that it simply is not meaningful to compare nations' education systems based on average scores.

The variability for Taiwan is particularly striking. Its average score, 285, is two points higher than that of Iowa, 283. Note, however, that Taiwan's 95th percentile is much higher than Iowa's—345 versus 330. And notice, too, that Taiwan's 5th percentile is much lower than Iowa's, 222 versus 233. I had occasion to ask a professor at National Cheng Chi university in Taipei why Taiwanese scores are so variable. He said it was because Taiwanese teachers concentrate their attention on able students and ignore less able students. That'll do it every time.

If we take the IAEP-2 scores for 13-year-olds in mathematics that have been converted to NAEP scores and merge them with the NAEP 8th grade mathematics data from the same year, we get some results, shown in Figure 7.3, that are even more surprising than the overall results.[3] Asian students in U.S. schools outscore their counterparts in both Taiwan and Korea. Even more startling, students in our more affluent suburbs outscore *everyone*. White students in U.S. schools tie Hungary, which finished third among countries.[4] Some might find it a bit surprising that Hungary would score so high, but Hungary has a long tradition of mathematics achievement. It finished among the top nations in an earlier math study as well and also in the Third International Math and Science Study released in late 1996 and discussed later in this chapter. Although at the time of the earlier study

---

[3] I have been criticized on occasion by members of the National Assessment Governing Board for this merging of data because not all of our 8th graders are 13-year-olds. In fact, not all of the tested students in other countries are 13 either, although that is how the study labels them. In addition, the NAGB assumption has been that these older students would score higher and inflate our average. In fact, NAEP data reported by age in *NAEP 1992 Trends in Academic Progress* show 13-year-olds scoring slightly higher than 8th graders. In this case, for example, the 13-year-olds averaged 292 while 8th graders averaged 285.

[4] Although the Soviet Union and Switzerland scored higher than Hungary, they did not have representative samples of students in the study.

FIGURE 7.3.

COMBINED IAEP-2 AND NAEP MATHEMATICS PROFICIENCY SCORES
FOR SELECTED HIGH-ACHIEVING STUDENT GROUPS.

Group	Score
Advantaged urban students, U.S. schools	292
Asian students, U.S. schools	287
Students in Taiwan	285
Students in top third of U.S. schools	284
Students in Korea	283
Students in Hungary	277
White students, U.S. schools	277

Note: "Advantaged urban" is a NAEP category, but it really *means* advantaged suburban.

---

only 50 percent of Hungarian senior-aged students were still in school, 100 percent of those were in mathematics classes. (For the sake of comparison, 82 percent of U.S. senior-aged students were in school, and 13 percent of those were in math classes; Japan had 92 percent in school, with 12 percent of those still in math. [McKnight, Crosswhite, Dossey, Kifer, Swafford, Travers, and Cooney 1987]).

In general, these results accord with a conclusion drawn by *Money* magazine in its 1994 comparison of public and private schools: if you live in a suburb and send your kids to private school, you're probably wasting your money (Topolnicki 1994). Asian and white students combined constitute more than 70 percent of the K–12 public school population. Thus, more than 70 percent of our public school students have an average mathematics proficiency score right up there with the top three nations.

Recall, however, that our overall scores were below the international average. If a large segment of our students are scoring high and our overall average is below average, some of our students must be scoring really low. And they are, as shown in Figure 7.4, which, like Figure 7.3, merges the IAEP-2 and NAEP scores.

FIGURE 7.4.

COMBINED IAEP-2 AND NAEP MATHEMATICS PROFICIENCY SCORES
FOR SELECTED LOW-ACHIEVING STUDENT GROUPS.

Group	Score
Students in Jordan	246
Students in Mississippi	246
Hispanic students, U.S. schools	245
Students in bottom third of U.S. schools	240
Disadvantaged urban students, U.S. schools	239
Black students, U.S. schools	236

Mississippi is not alone in scoring low among states. It is only in recent years that education has become a priority in the states of the Deep South, and that legacy shows up in these scores for most of the southern states. Beyond geography, however, much evidence points to poverty as the principal—though not sole, by any means—culprit in explaining the low scores of minority students.[5]

About 20 percent of white children live in poverty. This alone is more than double the proportion for most industrialized nations of Europe. But some groups in the United States are worse off, by far, than white children. For Hispanics, the poverty figure is 43 percent, and for blacks it is 53 percent (U.S. Bureau of the Census 1993).

At least one state superintendent I know has said "poverty is not an excuse." I was also taken to task by Stanley Pogrow in the June 1996 issue of *Phi Delta Kappan* for invoking poverty as explaining performance. Pogrow said my report on the above data in "The Fourth Bracey Report on the Condition of Public Education" "promotes the excuse that students who do poorly do so because of

---

[5] About 10 years ago, NAEP was moving to abolish ethnic categories because of a fear of racist interpretations of the data. They were dissuaded from doing so by Mary Hatwood Futrell, an African American who was then president of the National Education Association. Futrell acknowledged the danger, but argued that the categories should be retained because we needed to know if we were or were not making progress in the education of minority students.

demographic factors, such as poverty, that are beyond the control of schools. This is like arguing that we shouldn't expect to be able to fly because gravity is beyond human control" (p. 662). My response was as follows:

> No, it is not like arguing that at all. Poverty, like gravity, is a fact, a condition. Gravity acts on people in profound ways. So does poverty.
>
> "Poor children are more likely to have mothers who get late prenatal care and are more likely to be born too small. Medical studies show that poor children are three times more likely to have stunted growth, as a result of inadequate diets. Low-income youngsters are more likely to drown, suffocate, or be injured in a fire. Poor children are also about twice as likely to have physical or mental illness. Childhood death rates for poor youngsters are three times as high as those for other children. Poor children are seven times more likely to be abused or neglected" (Ohio Children's Defense Fund 1994).
>
> To overcome the effect of gravity and fly requires great effort. Men tried for centuries without success. To overcome the effects of poverty will require great effort, an effort we are not making (October 1996, p. 180).

Whatever the catastrophe, poor children are at risk for it.

We can see the direct impact of poverty on school achievement in Figure 7.5. To produce this chart, the researchers first divided students in high-poverty and low-poverty schools into categories based on what letter grade the children typically took home on report cards (Abt Associates 1993). High-poverty schools were defined as those in which 76 percent or more of the children were eligible for free or reduced-price lunches. Low-poverty schools were defined as those with eligibility rates of 0 to 20 percent. The researchers then looked to see how well children in the various categories performed on standardized tests of mathematics and reading.

As Figure 7.5 shows, children in low-poverty schools who got A's on their report cards scored about as well as one would expect on standardized tests of reading and math, in the 81st and 87th percentiles, respectively. Children in high-poverty schools who got A's

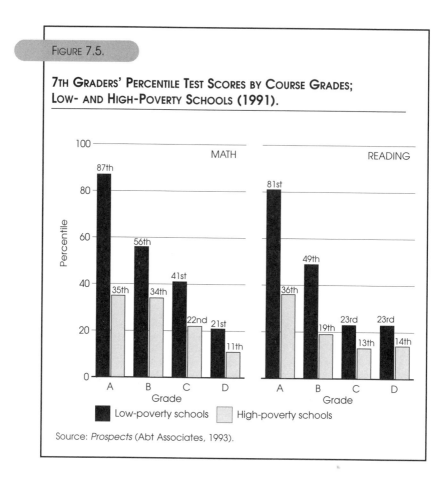

FIGURE 7.5.

**7TH GRADERS' PERCENTILE TEST SCORES BY COURSE GRADES;
LOW- AND HIGH-POVERTY SCHOOLS (1991).**

Source: *Prospects* (Abt Associates, 1993).

scored better than children in high-poverty schools who got lower letter grades, indicating that they are, indeed, the best students in these schools. But on neither test did the average scores of these *A* students reach as high as the 40th percentile.

In terms of international studies, we have no direct data such as those shown in Figure 7.5. We do know, however, that one study showed the United States with more than 20 percent of school-age children living in poverty *after* welfare and other social services were taken into account. This proportion was more than twice as large as that of any other industrialized nation in the study (UNICEF 1991). "I been poor and I been rich. Rich is better." Thus sayeth Pearl Bailey.

A study undertaken before IAEP-2, the 1987 Second International Mathematics Study (SIMS), has a somewhat different outcome (McKnight et al. 1987). The study focused on 8th graders. Among the 20 countries in SIMS, U.S. 8th graders finished smack in the middle on a test of arithmetic and slightly below average on a test of algebra. These results appear in Figures 7.6 and 7.7. The rankings on geometry and measurement were somewhat lower, 16th and 18th, respectively. The ranking on measurement is no doubt due to the lack of emphasis on this subject in U.S. math curriculums to this point.

As with IAEP-2, the scores of U.S. students are close to the international averages. The scores on geometry give a good indication of why mere rankings can be so misleading: students in the 4th-ranked

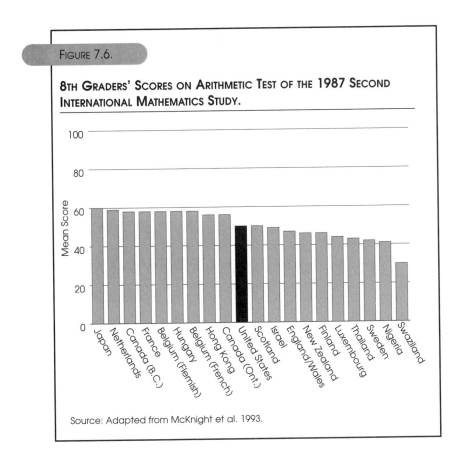

FIGURE 7.6.

8TH GRADERS' SCORES ON ARITHMETIC TEST OF THE 1987 SECOND INTERNATIONAL MATHEMATICS STUDY.

Source: Adapted from McKnight et al. 1993.

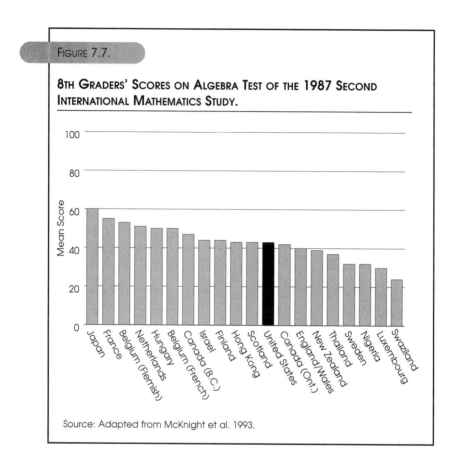

FIGURE 7.7.

8TH GRADERS' SCORES ON ALGEBRA TEST OF THE 1987 SECOND INTERNATIONAL MATHEMATICS STUDY.

Source: Adapted from McKnight et al. 1993.

country, Scotland, got only 6 percent more items right than the 16th-ranked U.S. students.

To some, the algebra results are quite remarkable. Although European and Asian curriculum sequences include algebra or pre-algebra for all students at 8th grade, only about 20 percent of American 8th graders take algebra or pre-algebra. (Whether we should begin algebra in 8th grade is another question. Most math educators I have spoken with think not, although they all agree that for most students, 8th grade math is a boring waste of time. But that is another issue). Ian Westbury (1992) at the University of Illinois, for instance, thought it would be interesting to see how U.S. students compared with the top-ranked Japanese students when the U.S. children were

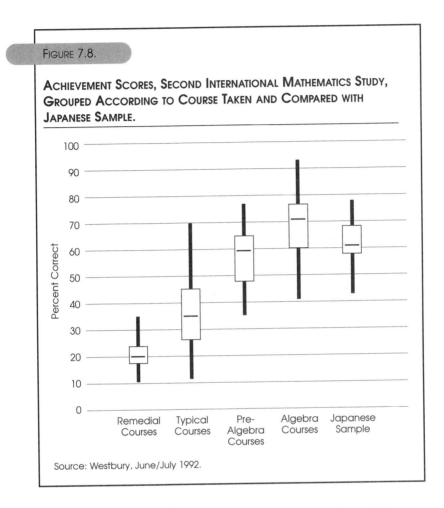

FIGURE 7.8.

ACHIEVEMENT SCORES, SECOND INTERNATIONAL MATHEMATICS STUDY, GROUPED ACCORDING TO COURSE TAKEN AND COMPARED WITH JAPANESE SAMPLE.

Source: Westbury, June/July 1992.

grouped by the type of arithmetic course they are taking. These results are shown in Figures 7.8 and 7.9.

An explanatory note about these figures may be helpful. These are called "box-and-whiskers" graphs. The horizontal line inside the box is the average score. The horizontal lines at the top and bottom of the boxes are some measure of variability—a standard deviation or the 75th percentile usually. And the "whiskers" extend to some extreme value—the 95th percentile, 99th percentile, 2nd or 3rd standard deviation, and so on. For the moment, let's concentrate just on averages.

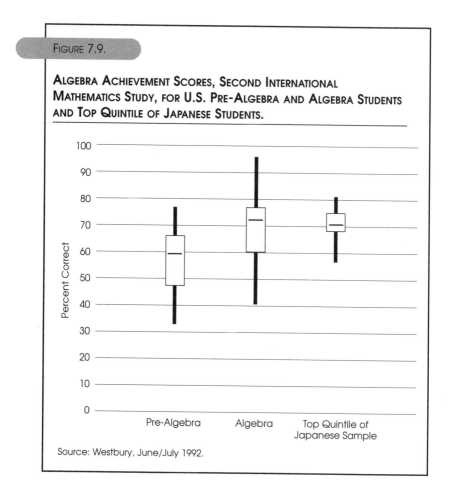

FIGURE 7.9.

ALGEBRA ACHIEVEMENT SCORES, SECOND INTERNATIONAL MATHEMATICS STUDY, FOR U.S. PRE-ALGEBRA AND ALGEBRA STUDENTS AND TOP QUINTILE OF JAPANESE STUDENTS.

Source: Westbury, June/July 1992.

As Figure 7.8 shows, U.S. students in typical or remedial courses do not compare at all well against Japanese students, but those in pre-algebra or algebra have scores quite comparable. Considering these data alone, however, biases the results in favor of U.S. students. The U.S. students in pre-algebra and algebra constitute about 20 percent of a grade, while the Japanese students are an entire age cohort. To take these factors into account, Westbury compared the scores of the U.S. students with the scores of the top 20 percent of Japanese students as indicated by the SIMS test. If we assume that the U.S. 8th graders in pre-algebra and algebra are the most able 20 percent in the United States, then comparing them with the top 20 percent of

Japanese students on SIMS renders a comparison among equivalent groups. As can be seen in Figure 7.9, the American students still score very close to the top 20 percent of the Japanese students. Contrary to the claim of Gray and Kemp noted at the start of this chapter, Westbury's study finds no evidence that America's best students "rank far behind" the best of other nations, even the best of the top-ranked nation overall, Japan.

Westbury's study reveals another noteworthy point: the standard deviations of the scores for U.S. students and Japanese students are quite different. Especially for the upper 20 percent of students, the variability for Japanese students is much smaller than the variability of U.S. students. This is not an accident. Whereas the United States is a nation that celebrates individual differences with slogans like "Be all that you can be," Japan is a country that tries to obliterate individual differences with folk sayings like "The nail that stands up gets hammered down." Studies of *ijime,* the bullying that occurs in Japanese schools, find that the children who become targets of bullying are different from the other children in some way.

The above discussion is by no means an attempt to put a happy face on the results of international comparisons in math and science. Whereas U.S. scores are consistently high in international comparisons of reading, they are usually below average in math and science.

One of the national education goals is to be number-one in the world in mathematics and science by the year 2000, and these results suggest the difficulty of attaining that target. Indeed, it is likely impossible. The impossibility does not stem from U.S. students' lack of ability. To some extent it comes from the quality of teaching in mathematics and science. But more than anything else, our failure to reach number-one status in math and science will likely have more to do with time than with anything else. Science instruction has been called "haphazard," and that seems as good a label as any.[6] Mathematics is more systematically taught, but research indicates that many elementary teachers are not as comfortable with mathematics as they

---

[6] In my daughter's elementary school, science facts were taught by the regular teacher, but when some kind of laboratory demonstration or experiment was called for, the assistant principal, the only male in the building, was called in.

are with reading. In one study, most teachers, when asked why a number cannot be divided by zero, could give no better explanation than "It's a rule"—if they gave any reason at all.

For these and other reasons, perhaps, elementary school teachers in the United States spend more time teaching reading than they do math and science combined. The results, as we have seen for math and science—and as we shall see shortly for reading—reflect the differing emphases.

The leaders in science and math scores are typically Japan, Korea, and Taiwan. The high scores of these Asian nations have led to visits by Americans interested in learning how they do it. The visitors have often returned gushing. Chester Finn virtually swooned over the Japanese accomplishments. Another member of the same visiting team, University of Illinois professor Herbert Walberg, was equally enthusiastic and thought that Japan's results could be transplanted here: "I think it's portable. Gumption and will power, that's the key" (Richburg 1985).

There is more wrong with Walberg's statement than its grammar. While considering the high test scores of Asian students, we should also consider how the systems produce them. Consider, for example, this excerpt from an article by Edward Desmond (April 22, 1996):

> Japan's public schools still produce consistently literate and numerate graduates. Nevertheless, a recent poll showed that 64 percent of parents distrust teachers and 67 percent are unhappy with the education their children receive. One apparent reason is the worsening problem of bullying, which has led to at least 20 suicides since May 1994. The problem escapes easy explanation, but most experts think it is rooted in the extreme conformity demanded in public school, right down to the pencils and schoolbags of children. Children who step out of line face merciless hazing, not only from students but also from teachers.[7]

---

[7] As a further indication of the rigidity, if a student does not have jet black hair, he or she must prove to the school that it was not dyed; if the hair is not perfectly straight, the student must prove it was not permed. A 1995 article by Susan Elbert, another American teaching in Japan, contends that *ijime,* which means "bullying," is not the right word for what is going on. She argues that *kurushime,* torturing, is more appropriate (Elbert 1995).

The most forceful indication that parents are disappointed in the public schools is the intense competition to get into private ones, from kindergarten through high school. The key to success is the *juku,* an evening and weekend cram school where children from the age of four prepare for college entrance examinations. Nearly 60 percent of junior high school students take *juku* classes, which cost their parents as much as $400 a month. They usually study material at least a year ahead of the public school curriculum and endure rigorous schedules that leave no time for the playground.

Akiko Tsutsui, a 10-year-old fifth grader, gets out of school at 3:30 p.m. and goes straight home to have a snack and do her homework. Three afternoons a week she leaves again at 4:45 for a *juku* session that lasts from 5:10 to 10:00. For almost the entire class, Akiko will listen to tutors explain how to answer test questions and will practice taking them herself. She sometimes attends all day on Sunday for extra help.

Competition in Japan has always been fierce and the schools have always demanded conformity and intense rote learning. But the system has become an extreme, decadent version of what it used to be.

Have a nice childhood, Akiko.

So, even though Desmond begins his piece saying that Japanese schools produce literate and numerate students, he concludes that the "key" is the juku. Many other observers in and out of the Japanese system concur.

If you think poor Akiko is losing her childhood, give a thought to little Moon Sae Bom in South Korea:

It was 11 p.m. and fourth grader Moon Sae Bom was solving math problems and double checking her social studies maps. For the past two hours, her mother had sat beside her, checking her answers, making sure the 10-year-old didn't fall asleep. This is a regular night in the Moon household and in millions of homes throughout South Korea, where mothers spend hours a day studying with their elementary school children, even plying them with caffeine to keep them awake and learning.

Today's South Korean students make the famously intense
Japanese students look easy going (Jordan 1996).

Time is not the only thing that Sae Bom's mother is spending. The article also claims that many South Korean parents spend 20 to 30 percent of their income for private tutors, and it cites a common Korean aphorism: If a high school student sleeps four hours a night, he will get into college. If he sleeps five hours a night, he won't.

What do the Koreans get for all of this sacrifice? Pathetically little. In IAEP-2, they did take first place in both mathematics and science (tied with Taiwan at age 13), but by a very small margin. Korean 9-year-olds got only 7 percent more items correct than the second-place Hungarians, and Korean 13-year-olds got only 2 percent more items correct than the third-place Swiss. Several other countries had scores quite close to those of Korea. In science, Korean 9-year-olds got 2 percent more items right than the second-place Taiwanese, and 3 percent more correct than the third-place U.S. students; and Korean 13-year-olds outscored the third-place Swiss by only 3 percent.

This, we should recall, was a study in which U.S. ranks were generally low; but even so, the largest difference between Korean and U.S. students was 18 percent more correct answers (for 13-year-olds in math), and the smallest difference was only 3 percent more correct answers (for 9-year-olds in science). If we factored in hours of study, the U.S. kids would, no doubt about it, score higher than the Koreans.

The results from the Third International Mathematics and Science Study (TIMSS) released in late 1996 are remarkably similar. This is perhaps the place to mention that the initial releases from TIMSS contain statements that might well be very misleading. The study reports that American teachers teach mathematics as much as or more than German and Japanese teachers, and they assign more homework than Japanese teachers.

It is true that American teachers spend more of the week in front of their classes—30 hours as compared with 20 hours for German teachers and still fewer hours for Japanese teachers. The analysis, however, does not tell what the children are doing when they are not being taught. Surely they are not just sitting there. Students in Japan and Germany, for instance, might well be working on materials that would be given as homework in the United States. While the TIMSS analysis quantifies how much time teachers spend teaching, it does not quantify how much time students spend learning. More important, so many of the Japanese students attend *jukus*—the private, after-hours schools in Japan—that Japanese teachers probably know that their charges have no time for additional work at home.

Sae Bom is lucky. Her mother plans to send her to high school in England, where, she has heard, children can be children. The Asian vision of childhood does not correspond to ours.

As David Berliner likes to note, we have a different vision of childhood, which includes working, dating, and hanging out at the mall (the article on Korean students reports that they have heard of such activities, but can't engage in them). We want our children to be able to do those things even though it is clear that working, at least, lowers our students' scores in the international comparisons. Whereas those who work fewer than 15 hours a week have higher grades than those who do not work or those who work more hours, a study by Richard Jaeger (1992) at the University of North Carolina at Greensboro found that the countries with the highest proportion of students with jobs also had the lowest test scores.

The articles excerpted above both appeared in the popular press and are, therefore, suspect in terms of how fully their observations can be generalized. But their conclusions have been confirmed by a number of Americans teaching in Asian schools and by researchers observing schools. Perhaps the most telling and thorough set of observations comes from Paul George at the University of Florida in a monograph, *The Japanese Secondary School: A Closer Look* (1995).

George's experience is likely unique. He had observed a class of youngsters for a full year while the children were in 7th grade. His son, Evan, was enrolled in the class, although his participation was limited because of his limited knowledge of Japanese. Then, when the students were seniors, George observed them again, also with Evan enrolled. George was able to enter numerous other schools in

Japan as well. The results he reports are startling and, to most Americans, would be alarming. Even George and his son were stunned: they took to using "eye signals to each other to express [their] mutual surprise, even shock, at what [they] were witnessing." Here's what caused the "mutual surprise":

> Japanese twelfth grade teachers adhered strictly to the direct instructional model . . . The ever-present influence of the university examination virtually guaranteed such whole class, direct instruction. Instruction focused almost entirely on lectures with occasional questions asked of students, drills, board work of the most traditional kind, and a limited number of other large group techniques.
>
> In spite of the ministry of education's continued insistence on the importance of individualized instruction, teacher-directed, textbook-centered, large group instruction was the only model used by teachers in any classroom, in any high school we observed. No small group work was ever employed during the period of our observation. No cooperative learning was utilized. No use of concrete materials, no active involvement of the students was in evidence. No media. No student work was posted. Bulletin boards that might add color and flavor to a classroom were also frequently missing or empty, leaving the classrooms with what American observers judged to be a bland if not barren look. No computers were utilized. No class discussion pursued. No students asked questions, ever. Even when solicited, student questions were few. Curiosity, clarification, or the expression of opinion or point of view was still not part of the educational process in the Japanese high school. It was the task of the teacher to put forth the national curriculum; it was the duty of the student to master it (p. 19).

The tension produced by the life-determining college entrance examinations in Japan is extraordinary. "The students talked about the examinations all the time," says Evan. The result of this tension is that the students cannot act in their normal ways. One student commented to George,

The students know from common sense that they should be quiet and polite, but they are so anxious about the coming entrance examinations that they cannot be quiet or sit still.

I am angry at the government because of this situation. . . . The students feel so bad that they want to kill themselves (here she quickly makes the suicidal gesture of *seppuku* [sword in the belly]). I also feel this way. The Japanese government is responsible for the suicides of so many students. The Japanese government is without sympathy for children (p. 30).

George continues his narrative:

Senior students were either bored enough to sleep, read comic books, and carry on conversational chatter; or so tense that they could not act in the polite and respectful ways that they knew to be correct; or both. Some senior students seemed quietly angry, discouraged, or alienated by their socially coerced participation in this process (p. 59).

I thought that the sleep George referred to might be indicative of the height of anxiety. One paradoxical response to extreme anxiety is to sleep. George said it was possible, but he (and others I've spoken with who have observed Japanese high schools) told me it was more likely sleep deprivation. According to George, the *juku* teachers tell the students not to pay any attention to their regular school, and students, having studied late into the night, then use class time to catch up on sleep.

George does not emphasize the emotional impact of the Japanese high school, other than its capacity to instill fear, but another American teaching in Japan commented on the extreme toll taken on social skills:

There is one important effect of Japan's education system that is not addressed: the incredible stunting of the students' social and psychological development. My students have all the emotional maturity of American elementary school students. If I ask a girl a question, often she will sink to the floor in embarrassment at being asked to answer a question. These are 19-year-old high school seniors I'm talking about. The boys aren't so dramatic; they just pretend that the teacher doesn't exist if they are unsure about things. Socially, these students are almost incapable of doing anything on their own. . . . I close with this comment: I consider the Japanese schools to be a national, institutionalized system of child abuse (Boylan 1993).

A national, institutionalized system of child abuse? This is what Finn and Walberg want to transport to the United States? These are bright, if misguided, people. How could they be so wrong? The answer, it seems, is two-part: (1) they weren't seeing typical Japanese schools, and (2) they didn't understand what they *were* seeing. Let's consider each of these partial answers in turn.

There is a natural tendency in all countries to show visitors only the best, not just in schools, but in all aspects of the culture. This tendency is writ large in Japan. In "The Fifth Bracey Report on the Condition of Public Education," I cited Japanese educator Kazuo Ishizaka on the problem of seeing reality. Ishizaka, head of the Curriculum Research Division of the Japanese National Institute for Educational Research, reports that he once took a group of visitors to what he considered to be an average Japanese school (one can almost see the mischievous glint in his eye as he reports the tale). "Oh, this is awful," he reports the visitors saying. "Why did you bring us here?" Because, he responds, visitors don't usually get to see the typical school.

In a telephone conversation, George was equally emphatic: "The high schools in Osaka are ranked from 1 to 27. As a visitor, you can get into 1 or 2; you probably can't get into 15 or 16. And even Japanese researchers can't get into 26 and 27." And maybe the people who run the international comparisons can't either: at one point, Ishizaka seriously impugned the representativeness of the Japanese sample in the Second International Mathematics Study.

The second part of our answer finds Americans looking at these good Japanese schools and not understanding what they are seeing. Harvard's Merry White, for instance, after examining the curriculum materials in Japanese high schools, declared that a high school diploma in Japan was the equivalent of a college degree in this country (1987). Ishizaka takes White to task (one can almost see him wagging his fingers at her) for this comment (1994). He tells her that one must be very careful to distinguish the *presented* curriculum from the *attained* curriculum. Many students, he implies, do not know what is going on in class.

Ishizaka's contention was echoed by Susan Goya, an American who has taught in Japanese schools for 20 years and whose children progressed through them (October 1993). Like Desmond, Goya also ascribed high test scores to the *juku:* "The secret of Japanese education is the *juku,* the cram school. Jukus are expensive, numerous and indispensable to the Japanese system of education. . . . *Jukus* survive because the quality of education in Japanese schools is poor" (p. 128). *The quality of education in Japanese schools is poor?* Sure fooled a bunch of naive Americans for quite a while. Goya is serious in her contention. She also says, "The fact is that Japanese public schools are doing a pathetic job of educating the people" (p. 128).

Like Ishizaka, Goya contends that U.S. visitors are fooled not only because they are taken to good schools, but because they don't understand what they are seeing. They see students in calculus classes, says Goya, and reasonably, but mistakenly, think that the students are learning calculus. But many of the students have not taken the prerequisites to that area of study. And "passing scores" on tests that admit students into calculus classes are as low as 5 percent correct. That's not a typo. There is no missing zero. That's 5 percent correct. "What observers don't seem to know is that upwards of 95 percent of the students do not understand what the teacher is talking about" (p. 126). No wonder they get anxious as the exams approach.

My own first-hand experience of education in Asia is limited to occasional guest lecturing some years ago at Hong Kong University. But my experience has been updated recently and extended to other Asian nations. On my first outing, following the way I had been taught, I prepared lectures for a class of advanced undergraduates in developmental psychology. The topic was Piaget, with an easy segue into the nature-nurture controversy. I also prepared some "leading" questions to stimulate thought and discussion. I did not know the phrase "wait time" at this point, but my wait time was pretty good. I had had some training in clinical psychology as well as experimental and knew it was important not to jump in just because a client was quiet. But the students in this class outwaited me. I asked questions. They sat there. Afterward, I asked the head of the psychology department, who had been in the room, what had happened. "Oh, they were probably embarrassed that you didn't know the answers." Even at the university level, professors dispense knowledge rather than stimulate thinking. I recently had occasion to ask a professor at National Ching Chi University in Taipei if my experience was still current. Yes, he replied, questions from professors are usually "met with stony silence."

The systems described do not sound to me like systems we would want to sentence our children to. And even if we wanted to borrow aspects from these systems, we should keep in mind that schools are embedded in a larger culture. That larger culture shapes them. Removing them from that context might be like removing a fish from water.

Even the Japanese, however, say they are trying to change their system. In a speech sponsored by the Education Commission of the States, Ishizaka argued that the very widening of education had had some negative outcomes:

> Radical social changes and the expansion of the quantity of education has left a great impact on the nature of education, and brought with it certain negative social characteristics as well, such as a society oriented toward human evaluation based on the single measure of the level of schooling attained, intensification of "exam hell" in preparation for entry into higher education, delinquent behavior among young people, and an extreme level of uniformity and inflexibility in formal school education (July 7, 1994).

According to Ishizaka, one part of the education reform efforts in Japan is an emphasis on

> principles such as respect for the individual, respect for individuality, freedom and independence, and personal respon-

100

sibility. In order to eliminate the adverse aspects of uniformity, inflexibility, and closedness which have characterized conventional Japanese education, it will be necessary to undertake drastic reforms of the contents, methods, and other aspects of education, based on this principle of putting emphasis on individuality.

Note that in an earlier quote, Paul George indicated that despite this emphasis on individuality from the ministry of education, nothing had changed in the classroom. Maybe the failure of top-down reform is a cultural universal.

We end this detour describing the characteristics of Asian education to return to the performance of U.S. students in international comparisons, the international study of reading mentioned earlier, and TIMMS.

The initial data from TIMSS were released in late 1996. As of this writing, the data included curriculum analyses for the 41 countries participating in the study and the math and science results for 8th graders. U.S. students scored just below average in mathematics and just above average in science. These results at the very least provide additional evidence that U.S. students are *not* "at or near the bottom," or "last or next to last" in such studies.

I hesitate to list the ranks of U.S. students in international comparisons for fear of heightening the "horse race" approach to them. Still, for the record, we can summarize the U.S. finishes in various international studies if only to show that the above characterizations are decidedly erroneous:

Second International Mathematics Study (SIMS), 1989

Arithmetic	10th of 20
Algebra	13th of 20
Geometry	16th of 20
Measurement	17th of 20

Because of enormous sampling difficulties, the 12th grade data from SIMS are not included, nor, for the same reasons, are earlier studies.

Second International Assessment of Educational Progress (IAEP-2), 1992

Mathematics (9-year-olds)   9th of 10
Science, 9-year-olds   3rd of 10
Mathematics, 13-year-olds   14th of 15
Science, 13-year-olds   13th of 15

How In the World Do Students Read?, 1992

9-year-olds   2nd of 31
14-year-olds   8th of 31*

Third International Mathematics and Science Study (TIMSS), 1996

8th graders, math   28th of 41†
8th graders, science   17th of 41‡

One major caution about the TIMSS data: The mathematics test contained 151 items, the science test, 135. Each test allowed only 90 minutes for completion. In contrast, the SAT contains 85 questions in the verbal section and 60 questions in the math section and allows 150 minutes for each section. We might want to consider what kinds of skills students actually demonstrate when they are asked to answer so many questions in such a short time (less than one minute per question for TIMSS).

It is worth noting that U.S. students' worst performances on SIMS were in geometry and measurement and that these results were replicated in TIMSS, though they are not displayed here. It is not clear why measurement is not part of the mathematics curriculum in the United States, but the poor showing in geometry is at least in part a historical artifact. Although most countries now keep more students in school through the secondary years, that was not nearly as true 20 years ago. If a nation felt geometry was important, it had to insert

---

* Statistically, could as readily be anywhere from 2nd to 11th
† Statistically, could as readily be anywhere from 21st to 34th
‡ Statistically, could be anywhere from 10th to 27th

geometric concepts into the curriculum before students started leaving (e.g., 7th or 8th grade). In the United States, however, dropout rates have been low enough for long enough that geometry could be placed in the 10th grade and largely ignored earlier without short-changing many students.

In a somewhat successful attempt to downplay the horse-race aspects of the study, the U.S. Department of Education showed the results in three categories: countries whose scores were higher than U.S. scores by a statistically significant margin, countries whose scores did not differ from U.S. scores by a statistically significant margin, and countries whose scores were lower than U.S. scores by a statistically significant margin. Thus, in mathematics, 20 countries scored higher than the United States, 7 scored lower, and 13 scored the same. In science, 9 countries scored higher than the United States, 16 scored lower, and 16 scored the same (the education reporter for the Associated Press told me that her bosses insisted that she rank the countries). Despite the rankings shown above, this is the proper perspective from which to view the results. The ranks for TIMSS are given solely to put the studies into a common metric.

Again, ranks and scores give a somewhat different perspective. In TIMSS, the international average score in math was 513, and the U.S. score was 500. In the same study, the international average in science was 516, and the U.S. score was 534. As in the reading study mentioned earlier, the scale used in this study is a 600-point scale identical to that of the SAT, with a mean of 500 and a standard deviation of 100. If we take the average score as the 50th percentile, U.S. students would fall at the 45th percentile in math and the 57th percentile in science (technically, this comparison is improper because we are starting with average scores—means—not medians, but the results would be very similar using medians).

Again, these results do not line up well with a national goal of being first in the world in mathematics and science on such measures, but neither are they cause for gnashing of teeth, for the scores of most countries are quite similar—more so in science than in mathematics. The top scorers were Asian nations, with Singapore appearing in a mathematics and science study for the first time and topping all comers in both subjects at both ages (Singapore participated in the 1992 IEA reading study and finished 11th). I do not know if Singapore has a system as harsh as those of Japan and Korea, though the stories related to the caning of an American student a few years ago suggest an overall totalitarian cast to the country.

It is true that the dictator of Singapore, Lee Kwan Yew, declared many years ago (he has been in power about 30 years) that education would be a high priority in Singapore. The population of Singapore is less than that of the Washington, D.C., metro area, so any pronouncement from a person in a position of total power would carry immediate weight. Lee also has offered incentives such as cash bonuses to induce highly educated couples to have more children. After the caning incident, Lee also suggested that Asian countries put forward a system of civil behavior not based on the Western canon, which he considers immoral.

TIMSS has the potential to be more valuable than previous studies because it contains curriculum analyses and, for a very narrow range, intensive case studies of actual instruction, including videotaped examples of teachers at work. Ironically, these analyses indicate that U.S. students might be stunted in part because, as noted earlier, teachers in U.S. schools teach more topics per year than teachers in other countries, which makes for shallow coverage. The analyses also show that the U.S. curriculum is about a year behind that in other countries and that U.S. teachers in math emphasize rules and procedures, whereas teachers in Japan emphasize conceptual understanding.

If these results can be discussed without negativity, they might actually benefit U.S. schools. It will be interesting to see what happens. The half dozen newspaper stories that I saw immediately after the release of the TIMSS results varied greatly in their coverage. The *New York Times* observed that American kids were "average." In *USA Today,* the headline read "mediocre." "Average" is a statement of fact, whereas "mediocre" is a judgment. The *Louisville Courier-Journal* devoted 15 of its 16 paragraphs to the below-average math scores, taking only a single-sentence paragraph to announce that science scores were above average. By reading only the headline and not the story in the *Washington Post,* one would conclude that TIMSS *did* find that U.S. students were "at or near the bottom." The *Post* story emphasized how far behind the Asian nations U.S. students are. Several stories had words like "fault" and "blame" in their headlines.

If one accepts the theory that a test's validity depends in part on its consequences, then the misreporting of these international comparisons is an overlooked aspect of their consequential validity and probably diminishes them seriously. Certainly the *New York Times* advertisement sponsored by the National Alliance of Business, the Business Roundtable, the National Governors Association, and others (discussed on page 76) would seriously invalidate the results of the Second International Assessment of Educational Progress.

TIMSS might have a chance of avoiding the negativity mentioned above. At this writing, none of the media heavy hitters have weighed in with any editorial comment, nor have any of their pundits. It might be that "average" news is no news. And for us in education, that might be good news.

As noted earlier, when a reading study appeared, not one media outlet reported it, even though a press release was prepared and distributed. Even *Education Week* missed it for two months. *Education Week* put the story on page one after then–*Education Week* reporter Robert Rothman received a copy of the full report from a friend living in Europe. *USA Today* picked up material from the *Education Week* article and also put the story on page one, complete with a quote from then–Deputy Secretary of Education Francie Alexander dismissing the results as irrelevant to the 1990s. (Recall that when this study appeared, George Bush was still president, and during his watch, nothing good would be said about public schools in the United States; when the Sandia engineers tried, their report was suppressed.) No other paper or electronic medium reported the story even then.

By November 1992, the story was appearing in other education periodicals, and it is instructive to look at how it was handled. The November 1992 *American School Board Journal* carried the story under the headline "Good News: Our 9-Year-Olds Read Well; Bad News: Our 14-Year-Olds Don't." The "good news" was that in a comparison of reading skills in 31 nations, only Finnish 9-year-olds scored higher than our TV-drenched couch potatoes. The bad news was that our 14-year-olds finished 8th.

In a letter to the editor of *ASBJ*, I asked how it could be that in a comparison of 31 nations, in which a 16th-place finish would be average, an 8th-place finish was "bad news"? It is still, after all, in the upper third of nations. More importantly, as with so many reports on these studies, the editors had focused only on ranks, not scores. If they had looked at the scores, shown in Figure 7.10, they would have seen that the 14-year-olds' performance put them as close to the top as the 9-year-olds were. The scale used is identical to that of the SAT, a 600-point scale with a mean of 500 and a standard deviation of 100. The 2nd-place 9-year-olds are 22 points out of 1st place; the 8th-place 14-year-olds are 25 points out of 1st, a measly 3 points further.

FIGURE 7.10.

U.S. RANKS AND SCORES IN 1992 INTERNATIONAL READING STUDY, *HOW IN THE WORLD DO STUDENTS READ?*, COMPARED WITH HIGHEST-RANKING NATIONS.

Rank and Nation	Score
9-Year-Olds	
1. Finland	569
2. United States	547
5. France	531
16. W. Germany	503
31. Venezuela	383
14-Year-Olds	
1. Finland	560
2. France	549
8. United States	535
11. Slovenia	532
16. W. Germany	522
31. Botswana	330

What's going on here? The answer is simple. For both ages, but especially for the 14-year-olds and even more so than in the math and science studies, the nations all have very similar scores. For example, the drop from France, in 2nd place, to the United States, in 8th place, is only 14 points. Indeed, statistical analyses by the National Center for Education Statistics revealed no statistically significant differences among the countries from 2nd-place France through 11th-place Slovenia.

This is quite a finding. The chance of finding a statistically significant result increases as the number of people in the sample grows. Many experiments in educational research use 25 to 40 students per group. In the international study of reading, student participants numbered no fewer than 1,500 per country and as many as 3,000. To not see *any* statistically different results among 10 countries indicates just how closely bunched the scores are.

During the 1994 Winter Olympics in Lillehammer, Norway, several discussions on television mentioned a Scandinavian taboo against standing out from the crowd. This shows up when we look at the highest scorers in the reading study. Although the Finnish average score is well above the U.S. average, the 90th, 95th, and 99th percentile scores of U.S. students at both ages were higher than the same percentile scores of Finnish kids. The best in the United States outscored the best of all 31 nations.

We can note here that West Germany finished in the middle of the pack. (The German scores were separated for East and West Germany to reflect the previous division of the nation, since the reunification was very recent when the scores were collected.) In a story about the study, the German Research Service expressed alarm over the results. "German standards were exceeded even in the United States" (German Research Service 1992). *Even.* German officials promptly blamed the low scores on families, saying they did not value books sufficiently.

One study by the U.S. Department of Education (1993) that looked at a number of international studies concluded that the more children are taught, the more they learn. As noted earlier, elementary teachers in the United States concentrate on reading, and U.S. kids rank first in the world in reading. If the teachers concentrated on math, math ranks in these comparisons would likely rise (and reading ranks fall).

People are concerned about math and science. (This worry has been voiced since the conclusion of World War II in spite of a chronic glut of mathematicians, scientists, and engineers; see Chapter 13.) To address this concern and to summarize the situation in this area, I offer a four-step program that will let U.S. kids beat the socks off Asian kids in math and science:

1. Convince U.S. parents that when their children arrive home from public school, they should feed them, then ship them off to a private school until 10 or 11 p.m. They should do this for elementary and secondary students alike. Most kids will have to attend all day on Sundays as well.

2. Convince U.S. parents that it is worth it to spend 20 to 30 percent of their income for this extra tutoring.

3. Convince U.S. parents that as their children approach their fourth birthday, they should take the kiddies on their knees and say, "You're going to be big boys and girls soon, so you need to start practicing for your college entrance exams."

4. Convince U.S. students that if they study and get four hours of sleep a night, they will get into college, but if they sleep five hours a night, they won't.

That'll do it.

In Sum

When someone says, "Our kids look awful compared with Asian or European kids," you can respond, "Not at all."

In reading, U.S. students were second in the world among 31 nations, and our 90th, 95th, and 99th percentiles were the best in the world. The best of the United States scored higher than the best of any other nation.

In mathematics, our *ranks* have often, but not always, been low, but our *scores* are very close to the international average. In one study, when the top 20 percent of U.S. students were compared with the top 20 percent of Japanese students on material both groups had studied, the scores were virtually identical. In another study, 70 percent of U.S. students had scores as high as those of students from the top three countries—Taiwan, Korea, and Hungary. Asian students in U.S. schools and students in advantaged suburban areas actually scored higher than students in any of these three countries.

Unfortunately, students in poor urban and poor rural areas did not score as well as did students in the lowest-scoring country. Poverty affects poor students in many ways, including achievement at school. Even students in poor schools who got *A*'s were found to score well below the national norm on standardized tests.

In science, the U.S. rank was high at one age level and low at another. In both instances, however, U.S. scores were close to the international average because the countries are tightly bunched.

Countries that outscore the United States in math and science have school systems on top of their school systems. That is, when the kids arrive home from the public schools, their mothers feed them and ship them off to a private school or a tutor. Some Japanese high school students often sleep in class because they are sleep-deprived and because their private school instructors have told them not to pay any attention to their public school teachers. Others are so anxious about the life-determining college entrance examinations that they cannot pay attention in class or even act civilly. Nevertheless, a recent article on Korean schools stated that in comparison with Korean students, Japanese students are "easygoing" (Jordan 1996).

Asian students are not taught how to think, just how to memorize. And, in spite of attending school and studying up to 80 hours a week, Asian students do not score much higher on tests of mathematics and science than do U.S. students, most of whom spend little time on homework.

Some of the enthusiasm for Japanese schools can be explained in terms of three reasons: (1) Japan has not provided a representative sample of students for international comparisons; it has chosen elite schools for these studies; (2) visitors from the United States have not been permitted to see even average Japanese schools; (3) U.S.

visitors have not realized what they were seeing. Observing students in calculus classes, they assumed the kids were learning calculus. In many instances, however, the students had not taken prerequisite courses or had "passed" qualifying examinations that had passing scores as low as 5 percent correct.

You can mention that Japanese education reformers have acknowledged that until recently, changes in society had produced "a society oriented toward human evaluation based on the single measure of the level of schooling attained, intensification of 'exam hell' in preparation for entry into higher education, delinquent behavior among young people, and an extreme level of uniformity and inflexibility in formal school education." This quote is by Kazuo Ishizaka, chief of the curriculum research department of the Japanese National Institute for Educational Research.

References

Abt Associates. (1993). *Prospects*. Boston: Author.

Boylan, P. Personal communication, April 1993.

Bracey, G. (October 1996). "REAR and Poverty." *Phi Delta Kappan* 78, 2: 80.

Desmond, E. (April 22, 1996). "The Failed Miracle." *Time,* 60–66.

Elbert, S. (December 7, 1995). "Education in Japan Intolerant of Departures from Rigid Norm," *New Canaan (CT) Advertiser*, p. B-17

George, P. (1995). *The Japanese Secondary School: A Closer Look*. Reston, Va.: National Association of Secondary School Principals.

German Research Service (November 1992). *Special Science Reports*, p. 12–14.

Gerstner, L.V., R.D. Semerad, D.P. Doyle, W.B. Johnston. (1994). *Reinventing Education*. New York: Dutton.

Goya, S. (October 1993). "The Secret of Japanese Education," *Phi Delta Kappan* 75, 2: 126–129.

Gray, C.B., and E.J. Kemp. (September 19, 1993). "Flunking Testing: Is Too Much Fairness Unfair to School Kids?" *Washington Post*, p. C-3.

Ishizaka, K. (1994). "Japanese Education—The Myth and the Realities." In *Different Visions of the Future of Education*. Ottawa, Ont.: Canadian Teachers Federation.

Ishizaka, K. (July 7, 1994). "The Progress of Educational Reform in Japan." Speech delivered to the Education Commission of the States Meeting, "Building Communities to Support Educational Change," Honolulu.

Jaeger, R. (October 1992). "World Class Standards, Choice and Privatization: Weak Measurement Serving Presumptive Policy." *Phi Delta Kappan* 74, 2: 118–128.

Jordan, M. (May 7, 1996). "School Bell Takes Its Toll in South Korea." *Washington Post*, p. A1.

Kelly, D. (November 7, 1991). "Defending U.S. Schools." *USA Today*. p. D-1.

Lapointe, A.E., J.M. Askew, and N.A. Mead. (1992). *Learning Science.* Princeton, N.J.: Educational Testing Service.

Lapointe, A.E., N.A. Mead, and J.M. Askew. (1992). *Learning Mathematics.* Princeton, N.J.: Educational Testing Service.

McKnight, C.C., F.J. Crosswhite, J.A. Dossey, E. Kifer, J.O. Swafford, K.J. Travers and T.J. Cooney. (1987). *The Underachieving Curriculum: Assessing U.S. Mathematics from an International Perspective.* Champaign, Ill.: Stipes Publishing.

National Center for Education Statistics. (1993). *Education in States and Nations.* Report No. NCES 93-237. Washington, D.C.: U.S. Department of Education.

Ohio Children's Defense Fund. (1994). *Helping Families Work.* Columbus, Ohio: Author.

Pogrow, S. (June 1996). "Reforming the Wannabe Reformers: Why Education Reforms Almost Always End Up Making Things Worse." *Phi Delta Kappan* 77, 10: 656–663.

Richburg, K. (October 19, 1985) "Japanese Education: Admired But Not Easily Imported." *Washington Post*, p. A-1.

Schoolland, K. (1990). *Shogun's Ghosts: The Dark Side of Japanese Education.* New York: Bergin and Garvey.

Shanker, A. (June 27, 1993). "Competing for Customers." *New York Times*, sect. 4, p. 7.

Shanker, A. (July 4, 1993). "Easily Imported." *New York Times*, sect. 4, p. 7.

Shanker, A. (July 11, 1993). "The Wrong Message." *New York Times*, sect. 4, p. 7.

Topolnicki, D.M. (October 1994). "Why Private Schools Are Rarely Worth the Money." *Money*, 98–112.

UNICEF. (1991). "The Progress of Nations." New York: Author.

U.S. Bureau of the Census. (1993). *Poverty in the United States.* p. 17.

U.S. Department of Education. (1993). *International Comparisons: What Have We Learned?* Washington, D.C.: Author.

Westbury, I. (June/July 1992). "Comparing American and Japanese Achievement: Is the United States Really a Low Achiever?" *Educational Researcher* 21, 5: 18–24.

White, M. (1987). *The Challenge of Japanese Education.* New York: Free Press.

The Dropout Rate

What do I say when someone says, "The dropout rate is awful and getting worse"?

Ironically, the worries over high school dropouts started only after dropouts became relatively rare. For most of this century, dropping out was so common that people didn't notice. In recent decades, however, the high school dropout became associated with crime and delinquency. In recent years, the dropout has become a source of concern because employers have required higher educational levels for good jobs (in some instances, even where such high education levels were not necessary for adequate job performance).

In Brief

In brief, you can say the following:

Dropout rates are improving and have been for a number of years.

We must admit at the outset that the dropout rate is one of the squishiest statistics we have in all of education. Different districts have different ways of determining dropouts, and districts vary in the conscientiousness with which they report such rates to state departments of education. Still, a number of studies by the U.S. Department of Education and by independent researchers have all produced consistent findings.

In Detail

Dropout rates can be defined in three general ways. The *event* dropout rate is the proportion of students who drop out in a given year. The *status* dropout rate indicates the proportion of the population who have not completed high school and are not enrolled in school. The *cohort* rate measures what happens to a single group (cohort) over a period of time.

Figure 8.1 shows the event dropout rates for whites, blacks, and Hispanics. As can be seen, the rates have been falling for blacks and whites (Office of Educational Research and Improvement 1994). Indeed, in 1992 black males had the lowest event dropout rate of all groups, although in 1993 it returned to earlier levels. For Hispanics the figures are somewhat misleading because they refer to all Hispanics regardless of birthplace. However, other studies have shown that Hispanics who arrive here from other countries are about three times more likely to drop out than are their peers born here. The various Hispanic groups also show substantial differences. Cuban American students drop out at very low rates, but Mexican American students have a high rate. Puerto Rican students and those from Central America fall in between these extremes. However, these results may well underestimate the proportion of Hispanic dropouts: reports abound that a number of Hispanic students in urban areas drop out before reaching high school and thus never enter the "official" dropout figures.

Indicators also strongly suggest that more and more students are what we might call "psychological dropouts," especially in poor urban areas. Ira Glass is a Chicago-based reporter for National Public Radio who spent two years observing first a high school and then an elementary school in the Chicago Public Schools system. I once recalled to him that former Secretary of Education William Bennett had called Chicago's schools the worst in the nation, and then asked him, "Is there any hope?" After a long pause he said, "If you could

FIGURE 8.1.

EVENT DROPOUT RATES FOR GRADES 10–12, AGES 15–24,
BY SEX AND RACE-ETHNICITY (1978–1993).

Year	White, non-Hispanic		Black, non-Hispanic		Hispanic	
	Male	Female	Male	Female	Male	Female
(percent)						
1978	6.4	5.1	11.0	9.5	15.9	8.5
1980	5.7	4.8	7.7	8.7	17.6	6.7
1982	4.9	4.6	8.9	6.6	9.5	8.8
1984	4.8	4.1	6.0	5.5	12.3	10.2
1986	3.8	3.7	5.1	5.7	12.4	11.3
1988[1]	4.3	4.1	6.3	5.6	12.3	8.2
1990[1]	3.5	3.1	4.2	5.7	8.7	7.2
1992[1,2]	3.5	4.0	3.3	6.7	7.6	9.0
1993[1,2]	4.1	3.7	6.4	5.3	5.1	8.0

[1] Numbers for these years reflect new editing procedures instituted by the Bureau of the Census for cases with missing data on school enrollment items.
[2] Numbers for these years reflect new wording of the educational attainment item in the CPS.
Note: Some figures are revised from those previously published.
Source: U.S. Department of Commerce, Bureau of the Census, Current Population Survey, October (various years), unpublished data.

really reduce class size, there might be, because a lot of students who are there aren't really *there.*" He thought that a drastic reduction in class size might give the teachers sufficient time to devise methods that might reach these psychologically absent students.

A recent report from Educational Research Service (1996) also documented increasing disengagement of even the better high school students, those who later went on to college. The results appear in Figure 8.2. This graph shows that the percentage of college freshmen who report that they talked with teachers outside of class, studied more than six hours a week, or belonged to student clubs has been declining over the past 10 years. The percentage of those

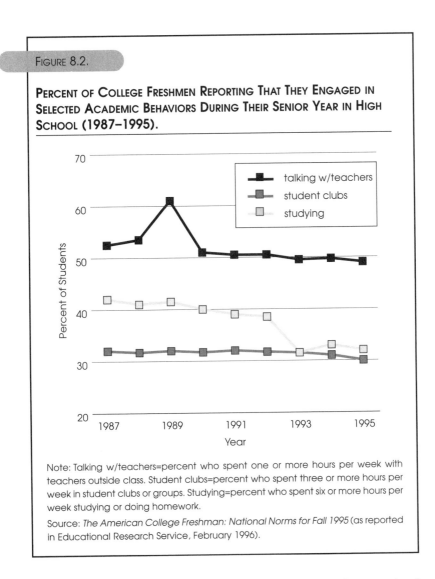

FIGURE 8.2.

PERCENT OF COLLEGE FRESHMEN REPORTING THAT THEY ENGAGED IN SELECTED ACADEMIC BEHAVIORS DURING THEIR SENIOR YEAR IN HIGH SCHOOL (1987–1995).

Note: Talking w/teachers=percent who spent one or more hours per week with teachers outside class. Student clubs=percent who spent three or more hours per week in student clubs or groups. Studying=percent who spent six or more hours per week studying or doing homework.

Source: *The American College Freshman: National Norms for Fall 1995* (as reported in Educational Research Service, February 1996).

studying at least six hours a week has increased in the last couple of years, but it is too soon to know if this is a trend or a blip.

Status dropout trends, shown in Figure 8.3, reveal a similar pattern. The dropout rate for black and white students aged 16 to 24 has been declining, while the rate for Hispanics has been generally high and somewhat volatile. The proportion of students who are status dropouts is highly related to income level. Students in low-income

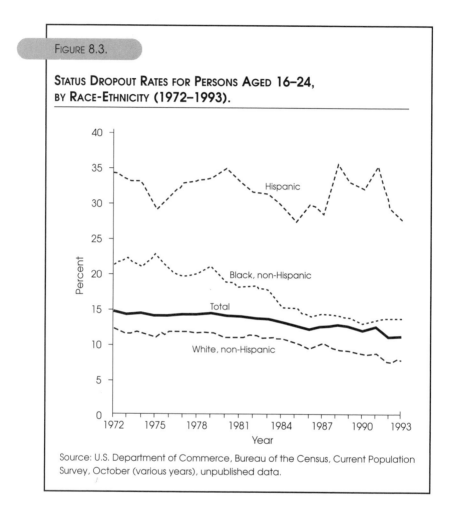

FIGURE 8.3.

STATUS DROPOUT RATES FOR PERSONS AGED 16–24,
BY RACE-ETHNICITY (1972–1993).

Source: U.S. Department of Commerce, Bureau of the Census, Current Population Survey, October (various years), unpublished data.

families are much more likely to become dropouts than are those in middle- or high-income families. At high income levels, Hispanic dropout rates approach those for blacks and whites. In these comparisons "high income" is defined as the upper 20 percent of incomes, "low income" as the lower 20 percent, and "middle income" as the 60 percent in between.

Cohort dropout rates, which come from two studies, "High School and Beyond" (HSB) and the "National Educational Longitudinal Study" (NELS:88), also show declining rates between 1982 and 1992. These results appear in Figure 8.4.

FIGURE 8.4.

HSB AND NELS:88 10TH- TO 12TH-GRADE COHORT DROPOUT RATES, BY DEMOGRAPHIC CHARACTERISTICS (1982–1992).

	Cohort dropout rate	
	HSB[1]	NELS:88
Status in 10th grade	1980–82	1990–92
Total	11.4	6.2
Sex		
Male	12.4	5.7
Female	10.4	6.7
Race-ethnicity[2]		
Asian/Pacific Islander	1.8	4.2
Hispanic	19.2	12.1
Black, non-Hispanic	13.5	7.9
White, non-Hispanic	10.2	5.0
Native American	26.9	17.0
Family below poverty level		
Yes	14.5	12.9
No	7.0	3.9
Family composition		
Intact family	6.4	4.6
Two adults/step-parents	14.5	8.2
Single parent	12.5	8.8
Other	21.5	10.9
Own child in home		
Yes	30.8	14.5
Male	15.9	7.7
Female	37.8	18.5
No	8.7	5.9
Male	9.3	5.5
Female	8.1	6.3

[1] Rates for HSB are revised from previously published data.

[2] Not shown separately are those included in the total whose race-ethnicity is unknown.

Sources: U.S. Department of Education, National Center for Education Statistics, High School and Beyond Study, Sophomore cohort, First Followup Survey, 1982, unpublished data. U.S. Department of Education, National Center for Education Statistics, National Education Longitudinal Study of 1988 First and Second Followup Surveys, 1990 and 1992, unpublished data.

Thus, the data for all three types of dropout rates show an improving dropout figure overall, except for Hispanics.

In Sum

When someone says the dropout rate is awful, you can say that it has gotten better over the last 25 years for everyone except Hispanics, whose rate remains high. You can also say that the overall rate for Hispanics is misleading because Hispanics who come here from other countries drop out at about three times the rate as do Hispanics who are born here. The dropout rate for whites and blacks is low. The high school completion rate for whites is 91 percent and for blacks, 82 percent—not exactly "awful" for either group, though there is room for improvement in each (OERI 1994). The "high school completion rate" is defined as the proportion of people age 21 and 22 who have attained a diploma or the equivalent. It is true that dropout rates in inner cities are much higher than in the suburbs. However, the prevalence of suburbs and the proportion of students in society who are white mean that the typical dropout is a white, suburban male. Inner-city dropout rates are not likely to change without massive infusion of resources.

There *is* a downside to dropout rates. Unpublished data I have received from Martin Haberman of the University of Wisconsin-Milwaukee show Milwaukee dropout rates rising in recent years. Richard Fossey (1996) also suggests rising rates in cities. If confirmed as a national trend, it would mean suburban rates are declining even more rapidly than national figures indicate. It would also be more evidence for our shameful neglect of urban schools.

References

Educational Research Service. (February 1996). "High School Seniors' Academic Engagement." *Educational Research Bulletin* 23, 6:1.

Fossey, R. (October 1996). "School Dropout Rates: Are We Sure They're Going Down?" *Phi Delta Kappan* 78, 2: 140–144.

Office of Educational Research and Improvement. (1994). *Dropout Rates in the United States, 1993*. Washington, D.C.: U.S. Department of Education.

Private Versus Public Schools

What do I say when someone says, "Private schools get better results than public schools"?

It is hard to address this contention directly, of course, because public and private schools differ in many ways. Private schools enroll and expel whom they please, whereas public schools admit everyone and do everything possible to avoid expelling anyone, tolerating behavior that no private school would (except those established to care for students with special needs). Private schools also differ enormously among themselves. Elite secular and church-affiliated college preparatory schools such as Andover and Choate *select* highly able students and charge enormous tuitions. These schools for the most part may be considered as one large ability group with an important difference: the students there look around the room and know that they are in competition with *everyone*. This no doubt increases their efforts.[1] Then there are parish Catholic schools, whose resources vary enormously. There are also secular schools established to avoid

---

[1] I don't know of any direct evidence for this at the high school level, but I saw it clearly when I was a teaching assistant at Stanford. Some 22 percent of each freshman class had never seen a B on their report cards, and they averaged about 1250 total on their SATs. Yet, according to administration guidelines for freshman classes, we were supposed to grade them on a curve that awarded 35 percent Cs and 15 percent Ds and Fs. They worked very hard.

racial integration. And so forth. In all, the characteristics of those attending private schools are likely to be different from those in the local public school.

In Brief

In brief, you can say the following:

• The differences between results in public and private schools are small, given the advantages of the private schools, except—
• Where there aren't any differences.

In Detail

If our only interest were in test scores, we would say that private schools do better than public schools. Figure 9.1 shows the NAEP scores in reading, math, and science for public and private schools

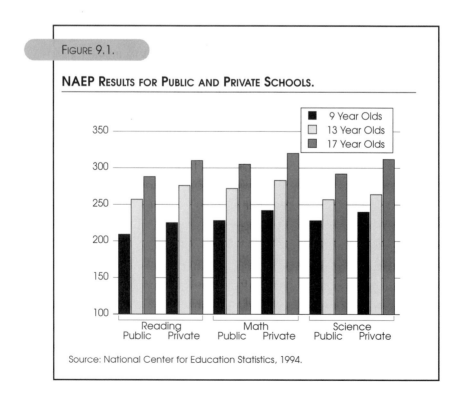

FIGURE 9.1.

NAEP RESULTS FOR PUBLIC AND PRIVATE SCHOOLS.

Source: National Center for Education Statistics, 1994.

(National Center for Education Statistics 1994). These are raw data that do not take into account differences in parental wealth or education level—two variables that make enormous differences in how students score on NAEP. Even so, the differences are not overwhelming. Translating the largest differences into percentile ranks, if the public school students had an average at the 50th percentile, the private school students would average at the 66th—not a tiny gap, but not overwhelming either. Translating the smallest differences into percentile ranks would leave the public school students at the 50th percentile and the private school students at the 55th.[2] As noted, these statistics are unadjusted for variables outside of school that favor private school children, including parental education and income levels.

Simply stated, children in private schools are significantly more likely to have highly educated and affluent parents. One study found that whereas 18 percent of public school parents had at least four years of college, 30 percent of parents with children in church-related schools had degrees, and 57 percent of parents with children in nonsectarian private schools had at least a bachelor's degree (Shanker and Rosenberg 1992). Conversely, the percentage of parents who had never finished high school was 8 percent for nonsectarian private schools, 10 percent for church-related schools, and 25 percent for public schools. This same 1991 study found that 27 percent of public school parents had annual incomes of more than $35,000. For church-related and nonsectarian school parents, the figures were 42 percent and 58 percent, respectively.

Figure 9.2, which shows NAEP mathematics scores of children in public and private schools whose parents have the same educational backgrounds, makes a dramatic point (Shanker and Rosenberg 1992). When parental educational levels are matched, there are almost no differences in public and private school children's performances. The only exceptions are for children of parents who either have not finished high school or who have not gone beyond the high school graduation level. In these cases, private schools have a slight advantage.

---

[2] This translation is made by dividing the difference between the two groups by the NAEP standard deviation and looking up the percent of area under the normal curve for the resulting quotient.

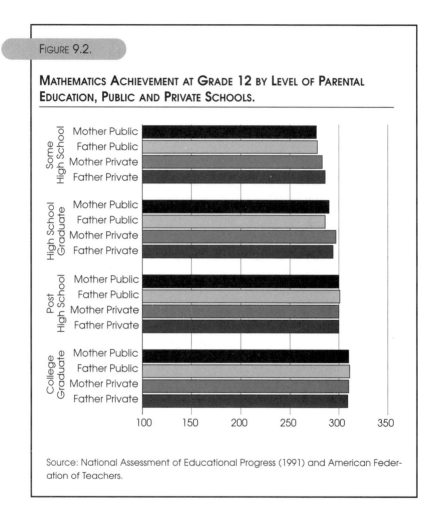

FIGURE 9.2.

MATHEMATICS ACHIEVEMENT AT GRADE 12 BY LEVEL OF PARENTAL EDUCATION, PUBLIC AND PRIVATE SCHOOLS.

Source: National Assessment of Educational Progress (1991) and American Federation of Teachers.

The data that purportedly show that private school students exceed public school students in their performance come from two analyses of the data set known as "High School and Beyond" (HSB). The first analysis was by James Coleman and colleagues (1981) and could not have arrived at a more timely moment to assure its impact. Ronald Reagan had entered the White House in early 1981 with a simple education agenda: get rid of the U.S. Department of Education, reinstall school prayer, and provide parents with vouchers and tuition tax credits that they could use for private schools. Coleman's report was published later in 1982. (When *A Nation at Risk* appeared, Reagan almost refused to accept it because, although it was highly critical of schools, it did not address any of these agenda items.) Bush continued Reagan's policy.

Coleman's 1982 report apparently showed that, even when background factors were taken into account, Catholic high schools got better performance out of their students than did public high schools (a small group of non-Catholic schools was initially included but later dropped because it did not represent secular schools in general). The Catholic advantage appeared in both a cross-sectional analysis of students at one time and a longitudinal analysis of the same students two years later.

Being misunderstood appears to have been a characteristic of Coleman's life. When his 1966 study appeared that looked at contributors to success in school, those who read—or at least looked at—the analysis came away claiming "it's all family" and schools counted for very little. Coleman actually said that his findings meant that we should spend much more money on poor and minority students.

Now in 1982, willing commentators—a little too willing—pronounced Catholic high schools superior by a considerable degree. Coleman, for his part, said, "One should not make a mistake: our estimates for the size of the private sector effects show them to be small" (p. 19). But he made that statement in a journal that only researchers read, not in a newspaper where it might be seen by laypeople. As it turned out, other analysts found the advantage to be even smaller than Coleman thought, and for some subject areas, it disappeared altogether (Coleman had looked at only reading, math, and vocabulary tests). A number of researchers found Catholic schools to do a little better in vocabulary, general mathematics, and writing. In reading, civics, advanced mathematics, and science, public schools equaled Catholic schools.

At the risk of sounding like we are making an excuse, we should note that a number of disinterested analysts have impugned the HSB tests because they showed so little change over the two years of the study, from 10th grade to 12th, for either public or Catholic schools. The tests seem to have focused largely on skills learned before high school, which wouldn't necessarily be *expected* to show much change. As John Witte of the University of Wisconsin observed, the gain from grade 10 to grade 12 was .2 standard deviation, while the learning rate in the first seven grades is closer to 1.0 standard deviation (1992). Given that high school is more content-intense than elementary and middle school, .2 standard deviation seems too little for a test that is measuring what is actually happening in the classroom. In addition, analysts have raised serious questions about the reliability of the HSB tests. In this light, the NAEP results seem all the more important.

We should note that it was not just "liberals" or public school champions who found Coleman's effect sizes small. Addressing the National Association of Independent Schools, Chester E. Finn Jr., a former assistant secretary of education under Reagan, an ardent advocate of choice, and soon-to-be charter member of the Edison Project and a charter school project from the Hudson Institute, said, "There's a differential, but it's a very small differential and, in an area where the public school performance is scandalously low." He then noted that twice as many private school as public school parents had college degrees:

> With differences that large in parent education, it is conceivable that there's no school effect showing up here at all. You [private schools] need to improve faster than the public schools if you expect to continue to have people paying an average of $6,200 a year for day schools . . . in order to get a presumably better educational product (Goldberg 1988).

The Reagan and Bush administrations followed an approach of never saying anything positive about public schools and accentuating the negative whenever possible. This strategy was designed to soften up the public to the idea of transferring public funds to private institutions. This hasn't happened yet, but the strategy did have some impact: when the second analysis of HSB data came along, nine years after Reagan began his first term and six years after *A Nation at Risk,* people were inclined to listen. The report, *Politics, Markets and America's Schools,* gained additional credibility because of the prestige of the sponsoring agency, The Brookings Institution (Chubb and Moe 1990). Although mistakenly labeled as "liberal" for a few years, Brookings has maintained a reputation for high-quality results devoid of the ideological drive that colors the reports of, for example, the Hudson Institute or the Heritage Foundation.

The authors, John Chubb and Terry Moe, argued that school effectiveness was due, in part, to school organization. Their argument goes like this:

> America's public schools are governed by institutions of direct democratic control, and their organizations should be expected to bear the indelible stamp of those institutions. They should tend to be highly bureaucratic and systematically lacking in the requisites of effective performance. Private schools, on the other hand, operate in a very different institutional setting distinguished by the basic features of markets—decentralization, competition, and choice—and their organizations should be expected to bear a very different stamp as a result. They should tend to possess autonomy, clarity of mission, strong leadership, and team cooperation that the public schools want but . . . are unlikely to have (p. 67).

This is straightforward. Would that the analysis itself had been the same. The analysis seems driven in part by what can only be called a rather zealous commitment to market-driven schooling through choice: "Choice is a self-contained reform with its own rationale and justification. It has the capacity *all by itself* to bring about the kind of transformation that, for years, reformers have been seeking to engineer in myriad ways" (p. 217). No wonder that Harold Howe at Harvard accused Chubb and Moe of treating choice as the eighth wonder of the world (1994).

Where are the transformational effects that have Chubb and Moe so in thrall? Did they find something in HSB that all of the other analysts missed? No, and many a researcher has spent many an hour trying to figure out what, exactly, they did do. No wonder that the press, disposed to say nasty things about public schools, was willing to utter positives about Chubb and Moe: there was no way that they could verify or refute how the authors had reached their conclusions. In *The Manufactured Crisis*, David Berliner and Bruce Biddle observe that Chubb and Moe "covered their tracks quite well, however, with vigorous rhetoric, extensive but slanted reviews of historical and comparative materials and—crucially—by drawing artful but questionable conclusions from analyses of HSB data" (1995, p. 120).

Rethinking School Choice: Limits of the Market Metaphor is a thoughtful, thorough, and fair elaboration of choice arguments and data. Its author, Jeffrey Henig, a political scientist at George Washington University, takes Chubb and Moe to task for using roundabout methods to obscure their major findings: that the gains between 10th and 12th grades are small and that differences between public and private schools are small (1994). In *School Choice,* Peter Cookson, a sociologist at Adelphi University, makes the same point:

> Their key variable, which they call school organization, is so comprehensive as to be incomprehensible. . . . The authors have so magnified their results by altering the unit of analysis from a score to a time frame, that they have lost sight of their own finding, which indicates that there are very few achievement gains between the sophomore and senior year. . . . I think it fair to say that Chubb and Moe's argument that student achievement is directly linked to school organization must be taken with an analytic grain of salt (1994, pp. 85–86).

Perhaps the fairest treatment of what is wrong with Chubb and Moe comes from John Witte:

> The Chubb and Moe study is anomalous in many regards. The empirical evidence they offer is drawn entirely from HSB. They disregard much of the prior research that established cautions, limitations, and standard practices observed by prior researchers using HSB data. Second, unlike other studies that base policy recommendations on inferences drawn from differences in achievement outcomes in public and private schools, *they never directly test the differential effect of public and private schools on achievement.* . . .
>
> They chose a circuitous research design and line of argument. . . .

Direct estimates of substantive relevance are difficult given the uninterpretable dependent variable they use. By making several simple assumptions, however, I estimate that, if one could modify a school's organization enough to move it from the median school, to the 84th percentile [of school organization], students in the school would, on average, get a fraction of 1 more item correct out of 115 items on the test. That is a small effect for an enormous change in organizational effectiveness (1992, p. 118, emphasis in the original).

Witte observes that when Chubb and Moe took to the op-ed pages of *Education Week* to respond to their critics, they did not challenge the critics' assertion that the differences between public and private schools are "minuscule."

Witte is also the principal evaluator of the choice program in Milwaukee, a program considered in more detail in Chapter 10, which is devoted to the issue of choice. Let us note here, however, that the private schools in Milwaukee have not proven to be more effective than the public schools in raising the achievement of low-income students. Witte's report at the end of five years of choice summarizes the situation as follows:

Outcomes after five years of the Choice Program remain mixed. Achievement change scores have varied considerably in the first five years of the program. Choice students' reading scores increased the first year, fell substantially in the second year, and have remained approximately the same in the next three years. In math, choice students were essentially the same in the first two years, recorded a significant increase in the third year, and then significantly declined this last year. . . .

Regression results, using a wide range of modeling approaches, including yearly models and a combined four-year model, generally indicated that choice and public school students were not much different. If there was a difference, Milwaukee Public Schools children did somewhat better in reading (1995, p. 14).

The Milwaukee Public Schools (MPS) have been maligned by some, but Witte thinks their students are doing better than the choice children. He notes in conversation, however, that it's a good-news/ bad-news tale. The choice and public schools start out with similar populations. As one moves through the grades, however, the public schools lose some of their middle-class, higher-scoring children. The private schools do not. That the public schools can keep pace with the private schools in spite of having an increasingly low-income clientele is quite remarkable.

In August 1996, a study appeared alleging that students in the choice schools in Milwaukee actually did show greater achievement than children in MPS; it just took four years for it to show up (Greene, Peterson, and Du 1996). The manner in which this "study" was launched reveals a great deal about the strategy of those advocating choice (see pp. 2–3).

The study is horribly flawed, although its rationale appears to make theoretical sense. In the Milwaukee program, schools that were oversubscribed[3] were required to select children at random. Thus, some children who applied for the program but lost out in the lottery for admission formed a control group demographically similar to those who applied and got in. This, the authors argue, formed the basis of a natural experiment: two groups chosen at random, one of which gets the treatment (admission to schools of choice), the other of which does not.

This is true. Or, rather, it *was* true when the study started. However, those in the control group of the study were only those for whom MPS could dig up test scores four years later. This was not many kids. Moreover, most of the children who were turned away from the choice program did not go to MPS but to other private schools. We have no way of knowing if those who went to private schools were like those who went to MPS. We do know that those who left the choice program over the years had lower test scores at the beginning than those who stayed, and this alone could create an apparent, but illusory, advantage for the choice students.

---

[3] Although the program has never been oversubscribed, some schools have been. Indeed, it is telling that 80 percent of the students in the control group came from only three schools.

Moreover, and more important, the experiences of the control group and the experimental group differed in ways that would create an advantage for the experimental group. The researchers implicitly acknowledge this. In explaining why the choice students took four years to show higher achievement, the researchers write, "The disruption of switching schools and adjusting to new routines and expectations may hinder improvement in test scores in the first year or two of being in a choice school. Educational benefits accumulate and multiply with the passage of time." Just so. But the control group kids were typical inner-city kids, meaning, in part, that they often experienced the "disruption of switching schools." The choice kids, by contrast, were in the same school four years running. If they enjoyed any advantage in achievement—and it is by no means clear that they did—the most parsimonious explanation for it has nothing to do with choice but with the stability that comes with being in the same school the whole time.

I have poked some holes in the study, and there are many more holes that I could poke (as I did in "The Sixth Bracey Report," [1996]) but we can note here that Alex Molnar (1996) of the University of Wisconsin has shown that even if you ignore every methodological flaw and every unsound assumption, the data still do not support the researchers' conclusions. The study is not a piece of research designed to inform the field. It is a piece of propaganda designed to influence policy makers, legislators, and others concerned with choice legislation.

Chubb and Moe contend that the restrictions imposed on public schools reduce their efficiency and their ability to experiment. And because they are a monopoly, they are not responsive to their clients, whether that be defined in terms of parents, children, or both. One wonders if Chubb and Moe have spent any time in schools. One characteristic that stuns Europeans who come here in programs such as the Fulbright exchange program is how *much* parents are involved in the schools and how responsive schools are. As Arthur Powell and his colleagues observed in *The Shopping Mall High School,* schools in the United States are a cacophony of curriculums and teaching styles (1985). Cookson, a longtime observer of the choice movement, states baldly that "from my research I would have to conclude that, by and large, pedagogical styles in private schools tend to be less imaginative and more 'chalk-and-talk' than in public schools" (Cookson 1994, p. 26).

And a study by Sandra Glass (1993) at Arizona State University contradicts the Chubb and Moe contention about public school restraints. From long interviews with administrators in public and private schools, she concluded that, although private school administrators don't have to work through local boards, both face similar kinds of pressures and constraints.

A less formal study by *Money* magazine reached a similar conclusion as did the above listed researchers. *Money* did not go into the ailing schools in poverty-ridden urban and rural areas. Its team looked at schools in suburbs and at a sample of private schools. Here's the summary:

> The best news to come out of *Money's* survey of public and private schools across America was that, by and large, public schools are not lacking in experienced topnotch teachers, challenging courses, or an environment that is conducive to learning. What many public schools are lacking is a student body brimming with kids eager to take advantage of what the school has to offer. But just because other kids disdain getting a good education doesn't mean a kid has to. Most teachers are dying for young, motivated minds to nurture. If they find an industrious student who is eager to learn, more often than not they will give him or her all of the personal attention that private tuition money could buy (Topolnicki 1994, p. 112).

If you live in a suburb and send your child to a private school, says *Money*, "Here's the bottom line: You are probably wasting your hard-earned money."

In Sum

When someone says private schools get better results than public schools, you can say, "not when parental attributes are equated." You can say that when the children of parents with the same level of education are examined—whether that level be high school graduate, some college, or college graduate—there are few or no differences in their scores on NAEP assessments whether they attend public schools or private schools. If parental attributes are not equated, there are differences in scores that derive from these differences in attributes. That is, parents who send their children to private school generally make more money than do public school parents, and money is correlated with test scores. Parents who use private schools also tend to have more education than do public school parents and, again, this affects test scores.

In addition to these parental differences, private schools have the luxury of selecting the children they want, whereas public schools must take all resident-eligible kids who walk in the door. It is also much easier for private schools to toss a disruptive student out of school. The differences between public and private school students on NAEP tests are not very large; given all of the advantages that private schools enjoy in terms of selecting kids and recruiting from among those with more educated parents, it is surprising that the differences are not large.

Indeed, in the Milwaukee program that gives a small number of parents vouchers to send their children to private schools, the program's evaluators concluded that the public schools were doing a *better* job than were the private schools.

You can call your commentator's attention to the *Money* magazine study of suburban public schools and private schools, which found that the public schools had more experienced teachers, challenging courses, and often more offerings than private schools. The editors concluded that if you live in a suburb and send your children to private school, "Here's the bottom line: You are probably wasting your money."

References

Associated Press. (August 14, 1996). "Choice Students Thrive in Private Schools." *New York Times*, p. A14.

Berliner, D., and B. Biddle. (1995). *The Manufactured Crisis*. New York: Addison Wesley.

Bracey, G. W. (October 1996). "The Sixth Bracey Report on the Condition of Public Education." *Phi Delta Kappan*, pp. 127–138.

Chubb, J., and T. Moe. (1990). *Politics, Markets, and America's Schools.* Washington, D.C.: The Brookings Institution.

Coleman, J., E. Campbell, C. Hobson, J. McPartland, A. Mood, F. Weinfeld, and R. York. (1966). *Equality of Educational Opportunity.* Washington, D.C.: U.S. Government Printing Office.

Coleman, J. (August/September 1981). "Response to Page & Keith." *Educational Researcher* 10, 6: 19.

Coleman, J.,T. Hoffer, and S. Kilgone. (1982). *High School Achievement: Public, Catholic and Private Schools Compared.* New York: Basic Books.

Cookson, P. (1994). *School Choice: The Struggle for the Soul of American Education.* New Haven, Conn.: Yale University Press.

Glass, S.M. (1993). *Markets and Myths: Autonomy of Principals and Teachers in Public and Private Secondary Schools.* Unpublished doctoral dissertation, Arizona State University.

Goldberg, K. (March 9, 1988). " 'Gravest Threat' to Private Schools in Better Public Ones, Finn Warns." *Education Week*, p. 1.

Greene, J. P., and P. E. Peterson. (August 14, 1996). "Good Choice Data Rescued from Bad Science." *Wall Street Journal*, p.A12.

Greene, J. P., P. E. Peterson, and J. Du. (August 30, 1996). "The Effectiveness of School Choice in Milwaukee: A Secondary Analysis of Data from the Program's Evaluation." Paper presented at the convention of the American Political Science Association, San Francisco, Calif.

Henig, J. (1994). *Rethinking School Choice: Limits of the Market Metaphor.* Princeton, N.J.: Princeton University Press.

Howe H. II. (1994). *Thinking About Our Kids.* New York: Free Press.

Molnar, A. (In press). "The Real School Choice Agenda." *Phi Delta Kappan.*

National Center for Education Statistics. (1994). *NAEP Trends in Academic Achievement.* Report No. 23-TR01. Washington, D.C.: U.S. Department of Education.

Powell, A.G., E. Farrar, and D.K. Cohen. (1985). *The Shopping Mall High School.* Boston: Houghton Mifflin.

Shanker, A., and B. Rosenberg. (1992). "Do Private Schools Outperform Public Schools? In *The Choice Controversy*, edited by Peter W. Cookson. Newbury Park, Calif.: Corwin Press.

Topolnicki, D.M. (October 1994). "Why Private Schools Are Rarely Worth the Money." *Money*, pp. 98–112.

Witte, J.F. (1992). "Public Subsidies for Private Schools: What Do We Know and How Do We Proceed?" In *The Choice Controversy*, edited by Peter Cookson Jr. Newbury Park, Calif.: Corwin Press.

Witte, J.F., T.D. Sterr, and C. A. Thorn. (1995). *Fifth Year Evaluation Report: Milwaukee Choice Program.* Madison, Wisc.: University of Wisconsin Department of Political Science.

Choice and Charter Schools

What do I say when someone says, "Choice is the only answer" or "Charter schools are the solution"?

As noted in the preceding chapters, recent years have witnessed presidents who promoted choice, along with studies that initially seemed to show that private schools outperformed public schools. That confluence, no doubt, helped promote choice. The concept of choice in education is hardly new, however. In his 1859 essay *On Liberty,* John Stuart Mill wrote,

> If the government were to make up its mind to require for every child a good education, it might save itself the trouble of providing one. It might leave to parents to obtain the education where and how they pleased, and content itself with helping to pay the school fees of the poorer classes or defraying the entire school expenses of those who have no one else to pay for them (p. 98).

Mill worried over the coercive possibility of state schools:

> It is a mere contrivance for molding people to be exactly like one another; and as the mold in which it casts them is that which pleases the predominant power in government, whether this be a monarch, a priesthood, an aristocracy, or the majority

of the existing generation, in proportion as it is efficient and successful, it establishes a despotism over the mind (p. 98).

Mill argued that "an education established and controlled by the State should only exist, if it exists at all, as one among many competing experiments" (p. 98). Mill's worries sound very much like the concerns voiced by those who opposed outcomes-based education and America 2000.

A century later, economist Milton Friedman "put Mill's analysis into modern economic dress" in his 1962 book, *Capitalism and Freedom*. Friedman used the schools to show the terrible things that happen when government has a monopoly on a service. The service should be open, in Friedman's opinion, to the forces of the free market. In the preceding chapter we saw how enraptured some analysts are with free-market operations.

In Brief

In brief, you can say the following:

• The results of choice experiments do not provide evidence that choice is an effective way, generally, of improving schools.

• When parents are given the option to choose, they choose on the basis of expediency—usually proximity—rather than on the basis of strong, highly rated programs. Choice works only when the consumer is informed, and as yet, the "consumers" of education don't appear to be very well informed.

• In countries that have implemented choice, private schools have siphoned off the more able students, leaving the public schools with increased problems and decreased resources.

• Where choice has worked, it has worked not because it has unleashed pent-up market forces, but because the much-maligned government and school bureaucrats have struggled hard to make it work.

• Surveys that show large majorities favoring choice are often misleading because of the way the question of choice is put to people. If asked, "Do you think you should have the right to send your children to a school other than the neighborhood school to which they are assigned?" most people will answer yes. But if asked, "Do you think that other people should have the right to send their children to your neighborhood school?" most people will answer no. In other words, I want choice, but I don't want it for you.

• Choice is a tool, one among many for improving schools. It is no panacea.

• As yet, no evidence shows that charter schools improve the learning of children in the charter schools, much less in the rest of the district. The jury is out on charter schools.

In Detail

First, we have to elaborate on the fact that "choice," although often presented as a simple alternative to "government schools," is in fact a complicated phenomenon. Long-time choice advocate (and voucher opponent) Mary Anne Raywid (1992) at Hofstra University has made a useful distinction among four kinds of choice or, more accurately, four reasons why people of very different political stripes have favored choice. Raywid distinguishes among education-driven, economics-driven, policy-driven, and governance-driven choice initiatives.

Education-driven choice initiatives base their calls for choice historically in the free-schools and alternative schools movement of the 1960s and early 1970s. These schools, often started with more enthusiasm than expertise, were supposed to free students from the arbitrary narrowness of typical school practice. The movement was given voice and legitimacy by two books of the early 1970s, Mario Fantini's *Public Schools of Choice,* and David Tyack's *The One Best System: A History of American Urban Education.* Fantini argued that different teachers had different ways of teaching, and different students had different ways of learning. Different students also differed in their interests and in the amount of structure they need. It didn't make sense to force them all into a single instructional model. Tyack, in contrast, looked at how the system had become uniform and the problems that such uniformity brought with it, especially in urban settings. Both authors focused on pupil choice; neither author addressed the issue of parental choice. Raywid herself has addressed both pupil and parental choice:

> There is no one best school for everyone. Accordingly, the deliberate diversification of schools is important to accommodating all and enabling each youngster to succeed. Moreover, youngsters will perform better and accomplish more in learning environments they have chosen than in environments which are simply assigned to them.
>
> There are many viable, desirable ways to educate, and no one best program can prove responsive to the diverse preferences a pluralistic, democratic society accepts as legitimate. Hence, the diversification of schools to accord with family value patterns and orientations is desirable (1992, p. 6).

Raywid's contentions assume that parents and students alike have sufficient information and wisdom to make wise choices. Free-market arguments rest on the same assumption. In some experiments, neither of these assumptions has been valid.

Education-driven choice is also the force behind a number of charter school advocates. People such as Joe Nathan and Ted Kolderie, both out of the alternative schools tradition, are charter school proponents who would ascribe to the rationales listed above.

The economics-driven initiatives for choice derive directly from free-market considerations. Currently, parents don't have the option of choosing alternative providers of education because of mandatory attendance regulations. The only alternatives available are private schools, which usually come with high tuitions and fees, rendering them effectively unavailable to most people. Like private monopolies, a public monopoly such as the school has no incentive to keep quality high and prices low. Indeed, it can use its monopolistic status to keep salaries high and working conditions undemanding while providing low-quality service. If a market-driven system were installed, good schools would thrive and bad schools would go out of business. That, anyway, is the theory. Reality is a bit more complicated.

Many people question whether the market analysis applies to schools. As Alex Molnar (1996) has observed in connection with charter schools, the underlying assumption of many free market advocates is that every human interaction can be reduced to a commercial transaction. Peter Cookson (1994) has written in a similar vein of the "commodification" of American life in general. In evaluating economics-driven choice, Cookson contrasts two metaphors:

> The first is that of democracy. At the heart of the democratic relationship is the implicit or explicit covenant: important human interactions are essentially communal. Democratic metaphors lead to a belief in the primacy and efficacy of citizenship as a way of life. The second metaphor is that of the market. At the heart of the market relationship is the implicit or explicit contract: human interactions are essentially exchanges. Market metaphors lead to a belief in the primacy and efficacy of consumership as a way of life.
>
> Schools may not transform society, but schools can transform the lives of children. For too long we have viewed education as a contractual relationship. The nature of this relationship is made most explicit by market advocates who speak of "educational products" as though education were something that could be manufactured and consumed. Learning is not something we can buy; it is something we must experience. (p. 99)

Thus, one response to economics-driven choice is to observe that it is profoundly antidemocratic. There is nothing democratic about capitalism. It is an economic system that coexists with democracy but does not inform it. Indeed, the fundamental drive of capitalism is totalitarian: capitalists at heart wish to establish a monopoly for their products.

Raywid calls the third type of choice "policy-driven." For instance, choice has been linked to the policy issues of equity. Rich people already have choice, the argument goes. They can choose where their children go to school by choosing where they live. Vouchers would give poor people the ability to choose as well. In addition to equity, choice is often linked to excellence. This link is most clear in the magnet schools movement, which attempts to establish excellent schools in poor areas to lure middle-class students. An assistant secretary of education, Mary Berry, once told reporters that magnet schools were a civil rights issue, not a school improvement issue. But advocates such as Ted Kolderie have seen choice more generally as a tool to create "the essential leverage for almost everything sought in the way of change and improvement in the schools" (Raywid 1992, p. 10). Raywid notes that this link is not always seen in real life.

Finally, Raywid describes "governance-driven" choice. Calls for choice coming from governance concerns reflect the worries of Mill noted at the beginning of this chapter. Schools under the control of individuals are preferable to those under the control of government because such schools are less likely to inculcate "official knowledge" in students. Stephen Arons, perhaps the foremost spokesman against this kind of orthodoxy, has noted that

> by requiring that the majority decided how all children should be socialized, we in effect require that people contest the most intractable issues of individual conscience. . . . The current structure of education in the United States is broadly inconsistent with the values advanced by the First Amendment (1982, p. 30).

The problem was captured in a *Time* magazine cover headline: "Whose Values?"

From these multiple considerations and drives have arisen a plethora of different kinds of choice: intradistrict, interdistrict, intrasectional (public schools only), intersectional (public and private), controlled choice (choice restricted by racial or socioeconomic considerations), magnet schools, postsecondary options (students can enroll at colleges at the expense of the schools), second-chance schools (alternatives for dropouts), charter schools, and workplace training. All of the above can be linked to voucher or tuition tax credit plans for financing them.

The above discussion summarizes the types of choice and the rationales behind each and shows clearly that the single word *choice* covers a multitude of activities. Choice also supposedly produces a plethora of benefits and evils, depending on one's position, and before proceeding to examine evidence, we need a good summary of what choice is supposed to do and what its opponents fear it will do.

Prochoice arguments include the following:

1. Bureaucracy will be reduced and those at the building level will have more autonomy.

2. Staff morale and motivation will improve.

3. Parents will be more involved because they are actively choosing a school, not being told where to send their children.

4. Schools will become more diverse, creative, imaginative.

5. Student achievement will rise as good schools thrive and poor ones disappear.

6. Making the schools subject to market forces will reduce costs and increase efficiency.

The first four of these arguments also undergird the charter schools movement.

Antichoice arguments include the following:

1. As schools are now stratified by residence, they will become stratified by achievement. A school can't grow like a business, and those that are favored by parents will be able to select the students they want. This will increase, not decrease, inequalities among schools.

2. The current distributions of students by race and class will produce inequitable choices and increase segregation.

3. Students served by existing special education programs will be less well served.

4. Accountability will be diminished. Standards might fall, too. Private schools will keep their methods secret and not divulge proper data about accomplishments or lack thereof.

5. Good information about the schools will be hard to come by. Schools will hype their programs and cook the numbers.

6. The common school tradition will be lost.

There is no way to really evaluate the choice or antichoice arguments in this country because most choice programs have been so narrowly focused. The experience of other nations, however, suggests that there are more negative outcomes than positive outcomes. We will discuss these later. Some evidence supports the fifth argument against choice. The rapid multiplication of charter schools may let us bring this argument to bear on them in the near future. Charter schools, by their charters, are supposed to improve achievement and may feel the need to say they have, even when they haven't.

Is there any evidence that the various plans actually produce the favorable outcomes? In general, the evidence appears weak. (Charter schools are too new to have produced data and are considered in a separate discussion below). Minnesota has a statewide choice plan, the only one of its kind. To date it has not served many people—less than 1 percent of the population as of 1996. Although a few parents are choosing schools on the basis of program reputation, most are picking a school in another district that is physically closer to their home than their "neighborhood" school is.

The most watched and certainly the most carefully evaluated choice program is that in Milwaukee. From 1991 through 1995, public funds have been provided for as many as 1.5 percent of the city's public school children to attend private schools. Church-affiliated schools have been included since 1994. The program has never in its first five years been anywhere close to fully subscribed. That is, more places are available in the schools than there have been children to take them. In addition, the turnover rate has been high. Evaluator John Witte thinks it might be no higher than that for Milwaukee public schools or urban schools generally, but if choice produced the good effects its advocates contend, it ought to show greater retention power. Witte's summary statement appears in Chapter 9.

That the private schools in Milwaukee were not able to improve the test scores of children coming to them from the public schools is puzzling. On average, no more than 72 students have ever chosen any given school, according to Witte's report (1995). One would think that such small numbers would not overwhelm a faculty and that the faculty ought to be able to find new ways to reach these children. But if, as Cookson (1994) contends, private schools are less imaginative than public schools, the lack of impact makes sense.

Jeffrey Henig's book *Rethinking School Choice: Limits of the Market Metaphor* contains a very complete review of the evidence available at the time of publication—1994. Henig finds that most of the "success stories" are either casual claims without real substance, studies with inadequate measures to demonstrate the claims, or studies so lacking in controls as to make the results impossible to interpret. Henig even finds so many flaws in the highly regarded Central Park East choice program in impoverished East Harlem that he worries the claims for its successes might be false.

In discussing where choice does work, Henig stands the market metaphor on its head. It works not because it unleashes pent-up market forces—which often cannot be seen—but because those who are maligned by the market theorists—the bureaucrats of schools and government—struggle hard to make it work.

> The expanded use of choice . . . is better understood as having arisen from collective negotiation, public leadership, and authoritative government, rather than from an unleashing of individual interests and market forces. . . . Whether reactive or activist, in all cases the process of experimentation [with choice] has been public and political—mediated through collective institutions and made to work through the application of authoritative government action (p. 150).

Authoritative government action? This is the very last thing the market-force theorists would predict. Indeed, it is the one thing that, in their view, should make things *worse*.

Looking at the experiences of specific districts, Cookson has this to say:

> When choice was being introduced in Fall River, the superintendent, other administrators, and teachers were out almost every night discussing choice with teachers, community groups, civic organizations, and community activists. Another key element in making choice work is to let the power flow to those who must own the choice program—the parents. Without parental involvement, choice cannot succeed (1994, p. 62).

How weird: it's the bureaucrats who make choice work.

And here's the kicker: in a market-based choice system, this public political experimentation, discussion, and debate, this discussion among educators, parents, community groups, and civic organizations would be hidden. In a market-based system, knowledge would be proprietary. A market-based system would deprive schools of one of their most important features: their openness to public scrutiny and debate. It is not only important for the public common school to prepare children for democracy. It is equally important for adults to be able to talk about it and debate its operations openly, democratically. European visitors to American schools are stunned at the participation of parents in the schools and at the responsiveness of schools to the parents—a responsiveness market advocates claim is not there. There is, truly, nothing else like it in society.

Cookson and Henig both come down on the side of choice, although in a much reduced role. Cookson calls it a tactic, not a strategy—one tactic among many. Henig calls it a tool, not a solution—one tool among many. Says Henig,

> A hammer can be an invaluable tool for some tasks and in some hands. But a hammer is no help in repairing a broken dish, and it can be dangerous if wielded in the dark or by a child. Those who use a tool have a responsibility to make sure that it is used when the time and the place are right. Because choice can have destructive consequences under some conditions, those who propose school choice as a policy priority have a responsibility to do the same. They also have a responsibility to consider other tools that might be available (1994, p. 205).

Henig then outlines situations in which choice, even choice that gives public funds to private institutions in some cases, might be useful. Just because the money goes to private schools doesn't necessarily mean that authority and responsibility for debate, deliberation, and decision making do too.

In evaluating negative arguments, we need to look to other countries that have applied choice on a grander scale than has been done in this nation. The results are largely what the skeptics would predict. Cookson (1994) reports that in Australia, the subsidization of private schools has resulted in private schools skimming off the most able students, leaving the public schools with less able students and establishing a dual school system based on race and class. In British Columbia, private schools, mostly Catholic, used public funds to raise salaries. But the use of public funds also brought a comprehensive state-required curriculum that imposed on the religious activities formerly attended to in the private schools. This left their constituents dissatisfied, but the schools found that they were "hooked" on the money and unable to reverse course. The support also did not lead to increases in diversity or innovations. As Cookson observes, when the private schools in Canada received public funds, they became similar to public schools—quite the reverse of what was supposed to happen.

Perhaps the Dutch experience is most instructive. Many government services in Holland are provided by small, private firms, many of which are church-affiliated. Public support for private schools has been available in Holland since 1917. To establish a private school, families, usually with the help of a church, petition the government. It sounds like what the free-marketers would want. But, as Henig noted, just because the money goes private doesn't mean the authority does. According to Frank Brown (1992) of the University of North Carolina, although experimentation is *possible* in Dutch schools, it is rarely seen, largely because all schools, public and private, must follow rigid government regulations on the curriculum.

All students must take exams at the end of elementary and secondary school. Parents "evaluate" the quality of the school largely on the socioeconomic mix of the students, not on test scores or other outcome variables. Parents base their choice of schools in part on this mix and in part on the schools' location: Catholic neighborhoods have Catholic schools, Protestant neighborhoods have Protestant schools. This reflects what in Holland is called "pillarization" and what in the United States would be called segregation by religion.

In recent years Holland has experienced considerable immigration from former colonies and an influx of "guest workers" from other countries. Schools that have experienced immigrant enrollment have experienced white flight as well. Indeed, it is common that once the student population of a school becomes 50 percent non-

Dutch, it soon becomes 100 percent non-Dutch. Recent Muslim arrivals have built their own schools in increasing numbers, adding to the "pillarization." Schools are not required to admit all applicants nor to use a lottery basis when they have a surplus of applicants. Long-established schools use the results from the examination that all students take at age 12 to select students, again creating an education system stratified by class.

Recent reports from Great Britain also are not encouraging for the free-marketers. Kathryn Stearns (1995), a Carnegie Foundation fellow residing in London, reports that schools that are popular—which she says are not necessarily the ones that are effective—do, indeed, thrive. But because the schools have limited opportunities to grow, they become first overcrowded and then selective. Middle-class parents use their choice options more than working-class parents do, but Stearns contends that this happens not because middle-class parents are more concerned with the education of their children. It happens because the working-class people are more apt to see the neighborhood school as central to their community. Contrary to market theory, none of the unpopular schools have closed; they simply do an increasingly poor job of educating a clientele that is increasingly difficult to educate.

> The gains for certain individuals have come at the expense of others and at the expense of the community as a whole. The legislation has led to increased social segregation and this, in turn, is leading to greater inequality of attainment. . . . If the British experience is any guide—and I think it is—abandoning the urban schools to the whims of the marketplace won't improve the lot of most students or the administration of urban education (Stearns 1995, p. A25).

Stearns's observation corroborates earlier and more formal research by others (Fitz, Edwards, and Whitty 1986).

CHARTER SCHOOLS

What, exactly, is a charter school? Nothing, exactly, but if Mickey Rooney and Judy Garland were around today, they'd probably shout, "Let's start a charter school!" Rarely has an unproven idea garnered such an enthusiastic response so rapidly among such a wide variety of political and ideological types.

For some, arriving from the political left, charter schools are the second coming of alternative schools and free schools. For others, arriving from the right, charter schools are a foot in the door for the choice movement. As Henig notes,

> Legislators and citizens who balk at full-fledged choice proposals seem to find charter schools less threatening, perhaps because they retain a clear role for government oversight; proponents of more extensive choice proposals seem to find charters an acceptable step in the right direction (1994, p. 232).

Through the charter movement, choice advocates have closed up shop in Washington (at least, for the time being) and opened up shop in the state capitals. Proponents have shifted from the White House to the state house.

Will charters lead to more extensive choice programs? Henig sees at least three ways in which this might happen. First, by ending mandatory attendance boundaries for at least some students, charter schools might make choice-based reform something more familiar, less threatening. Second, they might create new interest groups who become interested in pushing an expanded choice agenda. Third, they might provide evidence for the conditions under which choice actually leads to better education. Henig notes, however, that no matter what the reason for advocating charters, all

> show few signs of interest in systematic, empirical research that is ultimately needed if we are going to be able to separate bold claims from proven performance. Premature claims of success, reliance on anecdotal and unreliable evidence are still the rule of the day . . . (1994, p. 234).

Molnar echoes Henig, but is more skeptical and treats charters with rhetoric very much like that used to attack free-market choice programs:

> The struggle is not, at its root, between market-based reforms and the educational status quo. Rather, it is a battle over whether the democratic ideal of the common good can survive

the onslaught of a market mentality that threatens to turn every human relationship, inside and outside the classroom, into a commercial transaction (1996, p. 167).

As noted, charters are too new to have provided much data one way or another. The notion gained popularity after a speech given by Albert Shanker in 1988, and the first charter legislation, in Minnesota, was passed only in 1991. Charters *should* provide the requisite data because that is the whole idea: in return for a charter that reduces regulations and increases autonomy, the school promises to increase achievement. If it fails, the charter can be revoked. That's the theory. The reality is not as clean.

Naturally, with the charter hanging in the balance, schools will have some incentive to make the numbers look good. Mark Buechler (1996), however, contends that charter schools have mostly failed to specify the expected performance in any rigorous way and, consequently, "Charter schools' ability to improve students' achievement has yet to be proven" (1996, p. 1). Even a bulletin from the Hudson Institute, a frequent critic of public education and developer of a large charter school initiative, declares,

> We have yet to see a single state with a thoughtful and well-formed plan for evaluating its charter school program. Perhaps this is not surprising, given the sorry condition of most state standards-assessment-accountability-evaluation systems generally. The problem, however, is apt to be particularly acute for charter schools, where the whole point is to deliver better results in return for greater freedom (Finn, Bierlein, and Manno 1996, p. 7).

So watch for the data from charter schools, and evaluate it carefully.

The failure of some charter schools does not, in some people's view, mean the failure of the charter school movement. Quite the contrary. When the Edutrain charter school failed in California because of financial problems, free-market reformers hailed it as an example of the market imposing its discipline. But as Molnar points out, the market metaphor is inappropriate here. When a true market venture fails, the people who get punished are the people who invested in the venture. When Edutrain failed, the people who got hurt were the children who attended the school and whose lives were disrupted, and the taxpayers of Los Angeles whose money had been used to fund the enterprise. Says Molnar, "The charter school market feeds on the revenue provided by taxpayers even in failure. It is a market in which the financial risks are socialized and the financial gains are privatized" (1996, p. 167). The problem of Edutrain is a problem that advocates of choice, especially free-market choice, never address: How do you keep failing schools from hurting the children who occupy them?

The charter legislation in the approximately 20 states that have it varies enormously in the autonomy it grants or restricts. Not surprisingly, most of the charter schools have been established in the states that permit the most freedom. Of the nearly 300 charter schools in existence in 1996, more than 200 are in the five states with what advocates call "strong" charter laws.

According to theory, the success of charter schools will spill over to other schools in the district. Because we have no data indicating that the charter schools themselves work well, this widening of the circle of success cannot be assessed yet either. In some instances it is clear that the state will either have to increase its spending for charter schools or reduce resources given to other schools. In theory, again, this shouldn't happen because the students attending the charter schools lower the costs of the regular schools by lowering enrollment. Typically, however, the public school's costs are not reduced. Mrs. Johnson's 3rd grade does not pack up and head for a charter school, eliminating the need and therefore the cost of Mrs. Johnson. In districtwide plans, only a few children leave a given grade. The charter draws students from many classrooms in many schools, making savings impossible.

To date, charter schools have been forbidden to select students. If they have a surplus of applicants, they are supposed to admit by lottery. A study in California, however, found evidence of other selection processes. Whereas one goal of most charter schools is to increase parental involvement, some charter schools in California were requiring parents to sign contracts specifying that they would become involved in specific ways for specific amounts of time (Becker, Nakagawa, and Corwin 1995). The researchers uncovered some evidence that children were being selected on the basis of parents' willingness to sign the contracts.

It's too early to tell whether charters will be a lasting and profound educational reform or just another fad that quietly disappears in a few years. The failure of schools and states to plan for systematic evaluation does not bode well.

In Sum

When someone says choice (or charter schools) are the only way to improve our educational system, you can respond that neither alternative has proven itself yet and that the data on choice are not at all impressive.

Where choice has been established in the United States, the overwhelming majority of people have stayed with their neighborhood schools, and when they have chosen different schools, they often have chosen a new "neighborhood" school. That is, people often choose a school that is physically closer than their previous school but that had been unavailable because it was located in a different school district.

In the one choice program that has been adequately evaluated, the conclusion after five years is that the public schools are actually doing a slightly better job than the private schools. A thorough review of evidence reported in *Rethinking School Choice* found most claims in favor of choice to be overstated and underdocumented. Several observers have commented that where choice seems to have had a positive outcome, that outcome occurred because bureaucrats, who were supposed to be the problem, made it work.

You can point out that in England, which recently established choice, and in the Netherlands, which has a long-standing means of letting people establish choice, none of the outcomes predicted by free-market enthusiasts has happened, whereas a number of the negative outcomes predicted by critics have, in fact, occurred: schools have become more stratified by class, and the more educated have made more use of choice, leaving other schools to work with an increasingly difficult student body using fewer and fewer resources.

You can carefully point out that if schools become privatized, knowledge will become proprietary and not open to inspection. Schools will lose their openness to public scrutiny and debate.

When it comes to charter schools, you can say that the jury is still out: they are too new to really draw conclusions about, but their progress is not cause for optimism. Observers from the political left and right have both predicted that the schools will not collect the kind of data that they are supposed to according to their charters, that they will hype and overstate what numbers they do collect, and that conditions will be ripe for mismanagement and fraud.

Even those who suspect some of the motives of those in the charter school movement tend to approve of the idea of charter schools. They feel that too often in traditional schools the response to a proposed innovation is "It can't be done." Charter schools, at least, offer the promise of innovations within the public school system. Some of those promoting charter schools clearly want to improve public education in general, hoping that the effects of good charter schools will spread to other schools. Other advocates, just as clearly, see charter schools as the first step toward larger privatization movements and the destruction of the public school system.

References

Arons, S. (1982). "Educational Choice: Unanswered Questions in the American Experience. In *Family Choice in Schooling,* edited by M.E. Manley-Casimir. Lexington, Mass.: Lexington Press.

Becker, H.J., K. Nakagawa, and R.G. Corwin. (April 1995). "Parent Involvement Contracts in California's Charter Schools." Los Alamitos, Calif.: Southwest Regional Laboratory.

Brown, F. (1992). "The Dutch Experience with School Choice: Implications for American Education." In *The Choice Controversy,* edited by Peter W. Cookson. New Haven, Conn.: Yale University Press.

Buechler, M. (January 1996). "Charter Schools: Legislation and Results After Four Years." Indianapolis: Indiana University Policy Center.

Cookson, P.W. Jr. (1994). *School Choice: The Struggle for the Soul of American Education.* New Haven, Conn.: Yale University Press.

Fantini, M. (1973). *Public Schools of Choice*. New York: Simon & Schuster.

Finn, C.E. Jr., L.A. Bierlein, and B.V. Manno. (January 1996). "Charter Schools in Action: A First Look." Washington, D.C.: The Hudson Institute.

Fitz, J., T. Edwards, and G. Whitty. (1986). "Beneficiaries, Benefits, and Costs: An Investigation of the Assisted Places Scheme." *Research Papers in Education* 1, 3: 169–193.

Friedman, M. (1962). *Capitalism and Freedom*. Chicago: University of Chicago Press.

Henig, J. (1994). *Rethinking School Choice: Limits of the Market Metaphor*. Princeton, N.J.: Princeton University Press.

Mill, J.S. (1975). "On Liberty." In *On Liberty: Annotated Text, Sources, and Background Criticisms*, edited by D. Spitz. New York: W.W. Norton.

Molnar, A. (1996). *Giving Kids the Business: The Commercialization of School Reform*. Boulder, Colo.: Westview Press.

Raywid, M.A. (1992). "Choice Orientations, Discussions and Prospects." In *The Choice Controversy*, edited by Peter W. Cookson Jr. Newbury Park, Calif.: Corwin Press.

Stearns, K. (November 25, 1995). "School Choice: Survival of the Fittest." *Washington Post*, p. A25.

Tyack, D. (1974). *The One Best System: A History of American Urban Education*. Cambridge, Mass.: Harvard University Press.

Witte, J.F., T. D. Sterr, and C. A. Thorn. (1995). *Fifth Year Evaluation Report: Milwaukee Choice Program*. Madison, Wisc.: University of Wisconsin Department of Political Science.

The Global Marketplace

What do I say when someone says, "Lousy schools are producing a lousy work force, and that is killing us in the global marketplace"?

This kind of statement began to appear just after World War II. Then it was not the total work force that was so much a concern as the lack of foreign language speakers, engineers, scientists, and mathematicians that worried the critics. Suddenly the United States could no longer hide as an isolationist nation entering international conflicts only when absolutely necessary. Suddenly the United States was the only power not devastated by World War II with the capacity to challenge the Soviets for world domination. Previously schools had been recognized as important to the success of the individual. Now they were seen as vital to national security.

A Nation at Risk took this view a large step further (National Commission on Excellence in Education 1983). This document, a piece of propaganda that made incredibly selective use of data—when it used data at all—was basically a lie, but most of the country took it seriously. "What was unimaginable a generation ago has begun to occur—others are matching and surpassing our educational attainments" (p. 5). "Surpassing"? That was highly questionable, even when *Risk* appeared in 1983. But of course other nations were matching our attainments. What on earth did the authors of *Risk* *expect* other countries to do—lie around after the war and cede the number-one ranking in everything to the United States?

That other countries were now matching our attainments was important, *Risk* contended, because

> [t]he world is indeed one global village. We live among deter-
> mined, well-educated, and strongly motivated competitors. We
> compete with them for international standing and markets, not
> only with products but also with the ideas of our laboratories
> and neighborhood workshops. America's position in the world
> may once have been reasonably secure with only a few excep-
> tionally well-trained men and women. It is no longer. . . . If only
> to keep and improve on the slim competitive edge we still
> retain in world markets, we must dedicate ourselves to the
> reform of our educational system (p. 6).

This is all nonsense, but it was widely accepted nonsense. It is still widely accepted nonsense.

Risk generated a storm of criticism aimed at the schools. Soon it was followed by publications such as *America's Choice: High Skills or Low Wages!* (National Center on Education and the Economy 1990), which painted a grim picture of our economic position in the world unless we educated all people to higher levels (as we shall see, a more appropriate title would have been *America's Choice: High Skills and Low Wages!*). It was also followed by a recession that politicians and businesspeople alike blamed on the schools. The onset of the recession, unrelated to schools, gave *America's Choice* credibility it didn't deserve.

In Brief

In brief you can say the following:

• The U.S. economy is among the most competitive in the world. In 1994 and 1995, the Geneva-based World Economic Forum concluded that it was the most competitive among 25 industrial nations. In 1996 the Forum changed its formula for calculations and the United States "fell" to fourth place. The International Institute for

Management, another Swiss organization, prepared a list using a formula similar to the Forum's old one, and the United States remained number one. The Forum defines the economic competitiveness of a nation as "the ability of a country to achieve high rates of growth in Gross Domestic Product per capita."

- The U.S. worker is the most productive in the world.

- Although anecdotal evidence contends that businesses are concerned about "basic skills," national surveys find them actually concerned about attitudes: workers who don't show up on time or regularly, who don't interact well with other workers and with customers, who aren't positive about the product being sold.

- Schools have only a small impact on the economic well-being of the nation. This would not be true if the United States were a developing nation or if our schools were producing a generation of idiots, but neither of these conditions holds. The purported link between schools and the economy was exposed in an article in *Education Week* by Stanford's Larry Cuban as "The Great School Scam" (June 15, 1994). Cuban wondered why, if schools had taken the hit for the depression of the late 1980s, they had not gotten credit for the recovery of the 1990s. They shouldn't get credit for the turnaround, he concluded, but neither should they have been blamed for the recession. The definitive statement on the relationship between schools and the economy, however, had been penned earlier by Lawrence Cremin in his 1989 book *Public Education and Its Discontents:*

> American economic competitiveness with Japan and other nations is to a considerable degree a function of monetary, trade, and industrial policy, and of decisions made by the President and Congress, the Federal Reserve Board, and the federal departments of the Treasury and Commerce and Labor.
>
> Therefore, to contend that problems of international competitiveness can be solved by educational reform, especially educational reform defined solely as school reform, is not merely Utopian and millennialist, it is at best foolish and at worst a crass effort to direct attention away from those who are truly responsible for doing something about competitiveness and to lay the burden on the schools. It is a device that has been used repeatedly in the history of American education (p. 102).

You can ask your interrogators, "If schools are important to the health of the economy and Japanese and German schools are so good, why are both nations mired in longstanding recessions, the worst recessions, in fact, since World War II?"

• You can cite all of the data reported in previous chapters to refute the notion that schools are lousy.

In Detail

Let us elaborate on the first two statements.

Fortune magazine summed up the situation succinctly, if unaesthetically, on its March 1996 cover, which featured a picture of Federal Reserve Board Chairman Alan Greenspan and the comment, "It's *his* economy, stupid." That comment acknowledged the fact that Greenspan did more to affect the economy by raising interest rates 7 times in 12 months than all of the education reform since *A Nation at Risk*. Similarly, a June 1996 report on National Public Radio's "All Things Considered" noted that Japanese tourists visiting Hawaii were not coming there primarily for the lush scenery and silky beaches. They were coming to shop. They were coming to buy goods that either were not available in Japan or that were available at outrageous prices. If the United States is having a hard time competing with Japan, it's not because our goods are low quality. It's because Japan does not offer the open market that the United States does. Japanese business and industry can "compete" well with U.S. business and industry because the Japanese government either forbids U.S. goods from entering the country or slaps enormous tariffs on them.

This last was shown vividly in November 1996 at the summit of the Asian Pacific Economic Cooperation (APEC) forum. At President Clinton's urging, APEC members agreed to reduce and then eliminate the enormous tariffs these countries now put on U.S. computer hardware and software. *That* is how competitiveness gets altered.

The U.S. economy goes through cycles of expansion and contraction that seem virtually uncontrollable. People worry that the economy is expanding too fast and that inflation may start to increase. The Federal Reserve Board attempts to at least keep fluctuations in the economy small by adjusting interest rates. Whether this is the most effective or fair prescription for economic health is arguable. Many feel that wages are being kept artificially low because of the undue importance attributed to low interest rates. In June 1996, when the unemployment report showed that unemployment was at a 6-year low, the New York Stock Exchange lost 115 points. The U.S. economy—and its regulation—is strongly biased in favor of capital over labor. If unemployment falls much further, Wall Street worries that—perish the thought—wages might rise. It does not seem to worry, or even care, that maybe wages are being held to artificially low levels.

In any case, the economy has not paid much attention to the Marc Tuckers and Ray Marshalls of the world, and a good thing, too. Tucker was responsible for *America's Choice,* and a couple of years later, he and former Secretary of Labor Marshall coauthored *Thinking for a Living* (1992). In this book, they argued that the high-skills approach of *America's Choice* not only meant higher wages but full employment. They pointed to European nations as examples of countries that had moved further along than the United States toward the high-skills/high-wages definition of jobs. How they managed to overlook the extremely high unemployment rates in European nations is remarkable. Germany, which already has the shortest work week and longest vacations on the continent, is considering cutting the week more to give more jobs to more people. Italy and France are talking about job-sharing to accomplish the same goal. In late 1996, the unemployment rates for 12 European countries ranged from 6.9 percent (Netherlands) to 22.3 percent (Spain), with 7 of the 12 nations exceeding 11 percent unemployment; the U.S. rate was 4.9 percent ("What on Earth" 1996, p. A14).

At the same time, the U.S. economy is generating headlines such as "Now It's Japan's Turn to Play Catch-Up," "America Cranks It Up," and "The American Economy: Back on Top." In the last of these articles, *New York Times* economics writer Sylvia Nasar expressed typical sentiments:

> A three percent economic growth rate, a gain of two million jobs in the past year, and an inflation rate reminiscent of the 1960s make America the envy of the industrialized world. The amount the average American worker can produce, already the

highest in the world, is growing faster than in other wealthy countries, including Japan. The United States has become the world's low-cost provider of many sophisticated products and services, from plastics to software to financial services.

For the most part, these advantages will continue even after countries like Japan and Germany snap out of their recessions. It is the United States, not Japan, that is the master of the next generation of commercially important computer and communications technologies and also of leading-edge services from medicine to movie making (February 27, 1994, sec. 3, p. 1).

We need to emphasize several things about this quote. First, it was written in early 1994. By mid-1996 Japan and Germany had yet to snap out of their slumps. Somebody better go fix their schools (oddly, no one seems to have blamed their schools). Second, the U.S. worker is the most productive in the world. Study after study has shown this to be true. One study arbitrarily assigned U.S. productivity an index number of 100. Japan finished at 79, Germany 77. The authors of the analysis then took into account the number of hours worked in Japan, and its productivity fell to 58 (Levitan and Gallo 1991). We often think of Japanese industry in terms of gleaming, high-tech, postwar factories inspired and operated by the Total Quality Management theories of W. Edwards Deming. In fact, most of Japanese industry is an inefficient, mom-and-pop operation.

Third, the United States is the low-cost producer. Jobs in the fields named are not going overseas because they can be done better and more cheaply here. Did anyone actually believe that Honda, Toyota, Mercedes, and BMW chose their U.S. sites on the basis of schools? They chose them on the basis of cheap labor and tax breaks.[1] Ford runs what is said to be the most productive automobile plant in the world in Chihuahua, Mexico. It initially required workers to have nine years of education but has progressively cut back

---

[1] This kind of choice is based on different considerations than when companies are choosing where to relocate or build a new factory within the United States. In these situations, perceived school quality does play a role in determining where the factory is built.

on that requirement as skilled workers with less and less education showed they could do the job. Ford has discovered the difference between education and training.

An important point not mentioned in the above article represents the downside of this economic boom. It was captured well in a couple of political cartoons. In one, by Mike Keefe of the *Denver Post,* a college commencement speaker tells the new grads to "Go Forth and Serve Mankind"—and hands each a spatula for flipping hamburgers. In the other, by Jeff McNelly of the *Chicago Tribune,* an after-dinner speaker tells an audience, "The current economic recovery has produced 7.8 million jobs." At the same time, the busboy clearing tables thinks to himself, "And I have three of them."

McNelly's cartoon appeared just about the same time as a long article in *Time* titled "Working Harder, Getting Nowhere" (Gibbs 1995). The article made clear that McNelly's cartoon, however funny, had zeroed in on a nasty reality of the recovery: most of the jobs being created are in the low-paying service sector. Secretary of Labor Robert Reich and President Bill Clinton occasionally make comments to the contrary, but they don't press the issue, and they probably hope that no one is paying close attention.

Actually, that most new jobs are low-skill, low-tech, low-paying is a fact that not only is overlooked by our politicians but denied. On October 11, 1995, a letter signed by Bill Clinton and Al Gore in *USA Today* stated baldly that "by 2000 60 percent of all jobs will require advanced technological skills." Clinton and Gore did not specify what they meant by "advanced technological skills." I wrote them asking for a citation. I also requested the same information in letters to Reich and to Secretary of Education Richard Riley. I batted .250, getting one response for my four letters. An acting deputy assistant secretary of education told me she was certain that the Department of Labor would be able to answer my query.

Thus, I do not know where Clinton and Gore got their numbers. Clearly, they were not looking at reports provided by the Department of Labor. Figure 11.1 shows the occupations projected by the department to grow in number most rapidly from 1990 to 2005. Note that most of them are not really high-tech, nor are they all high-skill.

FIGURE 11.1.

10 FASTEST-GROWING JOBS IN THE UNITED STATES (1990–2005).

Occupation	Jobs in 2005	% Change from 1990
Home Health Aides	550,000	92
Paralegals	167,000	85
Systems Analysts	829,000	79
Home Care Aides	183,000	77
Physical Therapists	155,000	76
Medical Assistants	287,000	74
Operations Research Analysts	100,000	73
Human Services Workers	249,000	71
Radiologic Technicians	103,000	70
Medical Secretaries	390,000	68
Total Jobs: 3,013,000		

Source: U.S. Department of Labor, November 1991.

Note, too, that the top 10 fastest-growing occupations account for just over 3 million jobs.

It is important always to keep in mind the distinction between *rates* and *numbers*. If I make one dollar today, two tomorrow, and four on the next day, my *rate* of increase is proceeding quite nicely, but the *number* of dollars earned is small. Figure 11.2 shows the 10 occupational categories that will account for the largest *numbers* of jobs by 2005. Note that (1) the top-ranking job, retail sales, alone accounts for one-third more jobs than the top 10 fastest-growing jobs combined and (2) virtually none of these categories is high-skilled or high-tech or high-paying. When these projections were revised in 1995, they were essentially unchanged. The need for systems analysts is larger than ever, but so is the need for cashiers.

The conventional wisdom of capitalistic, free-market thinking contends that as jobs disappear from one sector, they are created else-

FIGURE 11.2.

10 OCCUPATIONS WITH LARGEST NUMBERS OF JOBS (1990–2005).

Occupation	Jobs in 2005	% Change from 1990
Salespeople	4,506,000	25
Managers	3,684,000	19
Janitors	3,562,000	19
Secretaries	3,312,000	8
Nurses	2,494,000	44
Office Clerks	3,407,000	25
Cashiers	3,318,000	26
Truck Drivers	2,979,000	26
Food Workers	2,158,000	34
Waiters, Waitresses	2,196,000	26

Total Jobs: 31,616,000

Source: U.S. Department of Labor, November 1991.

where. Around the turn of the 20th century, about half of all Americans were connected to farms. Now, fewer than 3 percent are. But the shift, although dislocating for individuals, produced no widespread unemployment in and of itself. Currently the conventional wisdom is being challenged, however. Richard Barnet, in an article called "The End of Jobs," reported, "I have visited a variety of highly automated factories in the United States and Europe, including automobile, electronics, and printing plants. The scarcity of people in these places is spooky" (1993, p. 51). Where are they? Workers in the manufacturing sector are the new farmworkers. Where are they going?

Jeremy Rifkin has extended this argument into a full-scale book, *The End of Work* (1995). Rifkin notes that the service sector has in recent years been the buffer for jobs lost in other sectors, but now technology is beginning to eat into the service sector as well. Bank tellers and telephone operators may have been the endangered species of past changes in automation, but smart technology is now producing fast-food restaurants that require only two people for their operation.

This trend might mean that the current obsession with the school-to-work transition needs to be replaced with a concern for the school-to-leisure transition. Rifkin, for one, certainly thinks so. People of all classes, he contends, are going to find themselves with a lot of time on their hands. How they use it, he thinks, might well determine the fate of the nation. He's not kidding.

In Sum

When someone says that schools are producing an awful work force, you can respond that study after study continues to find the U.S. worker to be the most productive in the world. In addition, schools have little to do with our ability to compete in the global marketplace. If Japan won't allow products into the country, we can't compete. If the president slaps sanctions on a country, competitiveness is affected. If the Federal Reserve Board increases (or decreases) interest rates, competitiveness is affected. Blaming schools for competitiveness woes is a common way of deflecting responsibility from those who actually have something to do with competitiveness. If we were a developing nation or if our schools were producing a generation of idiots, we most likely would not see the rising test scores and A-one performances in international comparisons of reading that U.S. students have achieved.

Even if there were a tight relationship between schools and the economy, there would be no cause for worry: the U.S. economy continues to be ranked the most competitive in the world. Beginning in late 1993, article after article in magazines and newspapers has contained glowing praise for the performance of the U.S. economy. Presidential candidate Bob Dole did not argue in 1996 that the economy was "broken," but that it could grow faster than it had under President Clinton.

To those who argue that schools and the economy are linked, you can point to Japan and Germany. These nations are often alleged to have better schools than the United States, yet both are mired in their worst recessions since World War II.

The schools have been doing an excellent job of generating a cadre of skilled workers—so much so that 30 percent of our college graduates have to take jobs that require no college. Business and industry have not kept their end of the bargain on the demand side. Most of the 10 million jobs that Clinton likes to crow about were produced in the low-paying service sector.

References

Barnet, R. (September 1993). "The End of Jobs." *Harper's,* pp. 47–52.

Cremin, L. (1989). *Public Education and Its Discontents.* New York: Harper and Row.

Cuban, L. (June 15, 1994). "The Great School Scam," *Education Week,* p. 44.

Gibbs, N. (July 3, 1995). "Working Hard, Getting Nowhere." *Time,* pp. 17–20.

Levitan, S., and F. Gallo. (1991). *Got to Learn to Earn.* Washington D.C.: Center for Social Policy Studies.

U.S. Department of Labor. (November 1991). "Job Projections." *Monthly Labor Review,* p. 81.

Marshall, R., and M. Tucker. (1992). *Thinking for a Living.* New York: Basic Books.

Nasar, S. (February 27, 1994). "The American Economy: Back on Top." *New York Times,* sec. 3, p. 1.

National Center on Education and the Economy. (1990). *America's Choice: High Skills or Low Wages!* Rochester, N.Y.: Author.

National Commission on Excellence in Education. (April 1983). *A Nation at Risk: A Report to the Nation.* Washington, D.C.: U.S. Government Printing Office.

Rifkin, J. (1995). *The End of Work.* New York: Putnam.

"What on Earth: A Weekly Look at Trends, People and Events Around the World." (November 30, 1996). *Washington Post,* p. A14.

Preparing Students for Work

What do I say when someone says, "Schools are not preparing students for work"?

Story after story and editorial after editorial bemoan the fact that students from U.S. high schools can't read, write, cipher, or sing. At a July 1996 conference, Governor George Allen of Virginia quoted IBM CEO Louis V. Gerstner as saying, "We can teach them job skills. What is killing us is teaching them how to read." This is a very convenient line for businesspeople to argue; if accepted, it requires the schools to do for free what businesses are currently paying for in on-the-job training. But actually, in spite of their laments, business in the United States invests a small amount for training compared with business in Europe and Asia—and then mostly for already skilled workers.

In Brief

In brief, you can say the following:

- Schools should not prepare students for work. Most work isn't worth doing, and schools should not collude with business to prepare students for occupations that are dull, boring, lacking in intrinsic value, and even dangerous.
- The U.S. worker is the most productive in the world, so what's the beef? (See Chapter 11).

- Projections for future jobs show that most of them will require extensive on-the-job training anyway.
- Thirty percent of college graduates currently take jobs that require no college. Schools have done a fabulous job on the supply side of producing workers, but business and industry have not kept up their end on the demand side.

In Detail

Earlier we mentioned the tendency among those pushing a variety of school reforms to see all human relations as commercial transactions. The press from business for more school-to-work activity is just more of the same. Having gotten control of the government, business now looks to the schools as the only thing left to dominate. Businesspeople often have a rather incredible notion of what they can get from workers and for what. And they are often disingenuous about their plight. In his farewell address, President Dwight Eisenhower warned us of the "military-industrial complex." It's time for a warning about the "government-industrial complex," which is even more frightening, as the government has a great deal of control over what the media report. That is not a paranoid statement. Studies show that most of what journalists write is what people in positions of authority tell them to write. Truly skeptical, investigative journalism is rare.

As an example of disingenuousness, take, for instance, the commentary of Alan Wurtzel, chairman of the board of Circuit City, a large discount electronics firm. Wurtzel (1993) took to the op-ed page of the *Washington Post* to bemoan the nature of high school graduates, a group that Wurtzel said his firm seldom hired. Said Wurtzel, "In hiring new employees for our stores and warehouses, Circuit City is looking for people who are able to provide very high levels of customer service, who are honest, and who have a positive, enthusiastic, achievement-oriented work ethic." I wondered what workers with all of these fine qualities—apparently found only in college grads—cost Wurtzel. The Circuit City personnel department told me that the people who work in the warehouses get $4.25 an hour, the minimum wage at the time of my inquiry, and the sales force works strictly for commission.

In a similar vein, Pacific Telesis CEO Sam Ginn regaled audiences with the tale of how his company gave a reading test to 6,400 potential employees, and only 2,800 of them scored high enough that he would feel comfortable hiring them (Rothstein 1993). What Ginn did not tell audiences is that his jobs paid only $7.00 an hour. That might sound like a lot to those of us who grew up making 50 to 75 cents an hour, but projected over a 40-hour work week and a 50-week year, it's only $14,000 a year. Did Ginn really think that America's literati were going to show up to apply for such jobs? Why, we pay even teachers more than that.

Moreover, Ginn did not tell his audiences that he had only 700 jobs—his test had four times as many qualified applicants as jobs. Wurtzel's and Ginn's attitude was captured in a "Frank and Ernest" cartoon. A personnel director tells them, "What we want is someone who is smart enough to pass our aptitude test and dumb enough to work for what we pay."

The fact is, schools have done a fabulous job on the supply side of jobs. Business and industry have done a lousy job on the demand side. Currently, about 30 percent of college graduates take jobs that require no college. As more and more students go to college and as more and more low-paying, low-skill jobs are created, this problem will only increase. The same projections from the Department of Labor showing that most jobs in the future will be low-tech and low-skill (see Chapter 11) also show that whereas jobs requiring a college education will increase faster than those that don't, the greatest increase will be in jobs that, whatever education level they require, call for extensive on-the-job training (Bureau of Labor Statistics 1995). Even if this weren't true, research on the nature of generalization and transfer of skills would indicate that there is little that schools can do to prepare students for specific occupations.

Not until the second decade of the 20th century did schools begin to concern themselves with jobs. The curriculum of the high school was the curriculum needed to enter colleges and universities, even though only a tiny proportion of high school graduates attended college. Schools were more concerned about the civic function of education as described by Thomas Jefferson in 1732. Jefferson saw education as a means of protecting us from *our* government:

> In every government on earth is some trace of human weakness, some germ of corruption and degeneracy which cunning will discover, and weakness insensibly open, cultivate and improve. Every government degenerates when trusted to the rulers over the people alone. The people themselves therefore are its only safe depositories. And to rend even them safe, their minds must be improved somewhat (1978, p. 11).

Schools would do well to attend more to this civic function. In addition, they would do well to attend more to the school-to-leisure transition mentioned at the end of Chapter 11.

We used to make fun of the communists and their "glorious worker" propaganda, but we glorify work just as propagandistically. We're just more subtle about it. We put all jobs under the one rubric of work, which then allows us to forget how dreadful much work really is. Should schools really help prepare students to endure the boredom of meaningless, small, repetitive, dull, *unhealthy* tasks? Work is often as nasty as it is unavoidable, and we should realize that and treat it appropriately, not pretend it is something wonderful.

The comic strip "Dilbert" captures the world of work, at least the white-collar world. The strip is something of a phenomenon in itself: already seen in more than 800 newspapers nationally, it is still the fastest-growing strip in the country. Dilbert works in some place that produces something, apparently badly. The employees are constantly inventing ways of conning each other and the customers. The firm is inhabited by inept managers and conniving accountants. Kafka would love it. In one segment, Dilbert proposes to a coworker that they quit and start their own business. "Why quit?" asks the coworker. "We can run our new company from our cubicles and get paid too." Dilbert asks, "Wouldn't that be immoral?" The coworker replies, "That's only an issue for people who aren't already in hell."

Apparently, a lot of workers in this country think they're already in hell. Dilbert's creator, Scott Adams, put his Internet address on the strip some years ago. Since that time, he has been besieged by letters asking, "How did you find out where I worked?"

In Sum

When someone says schools are not preparing students for the world of work, one available response is that they should *not* prepare students for the world of work. It is the business of business to train workers. Much work isn't worth doing, is dull, boring, even dangerous. Schools should not collude with business to prepare kids to endure carpal tunnel syndrome and similar ills.

If you are uncomfortable with this position—and business has come to so dominate the thinking about schools that many people might be—other retorts are available. The first can be stated in terms of the U.S. worker, consistently found to be the most productive in the world in spite of the fact that business and industry—although they claim otherwise—do not spend a lot of money on training.

You can also mention that the research on transfer of skills indicates that it would be impossible for schools to prepare students for particular jobs. As information technology leads to the rapid obsolescence of specific jobs and the creation of new ones for which skills cannot be specified in advance, job training in the public schools becomes even more unlikely.

You can also say that projections from the Bureau of Labor Statistics indicate that most jobs in the future will require extended periods of on-the-job training no matter what level of education they require. Business and industry need to get used to dealing with rapid change.

References

Bureau of Labor Statistics. (1995). *Employment Outlook, 1994–2005.* Washington D.C.: Author.

Jefferson, T. (1978). "An Education Plan for Virginia." In *In Defense of the American Public School,* edited by Arthur J. Newman. Berkeley, Calif.: Schenkman Publishing.

Rothstein, R. (Spring 1993). "The Myth of Public School Failure." *American Prospect* 13, 3:20–24.

Wurtzel, A. (December 7, 1993). "Getting from School to Work." *Washington Post,* p. A25.

The Shortage of Scientists

What do I say when someone says, "We have or will have a shortage of scientists, mathematicians, and engineers"?

As noted in Chapter 11, this myth was born and came to the fore shortly after World War II, when it was feared that the Soviet Union would outstrip us in both ideological and technological advances. Admiral Hyman Rickover, often called the father of the nuclear navy, traveled the country armed with numbers provided by CIA Chief Allen Dulles that indicated the Soviet Union would produce 1.2 million scientists and engineers in the same period that we would produce "only" 900,000. The Soviet Union, it is now clear, threw resources at its military machine in ways that devastated both its economy and its ecology. And it never outstripped us. In any case, the shortage myth has not been true for some time, if it ever was.

In Brief

In brief, you can say the following:

• We have a surplus of scientists, mathematicians, and engineers. The projections of shortages were a ploy to obtain more money for the National Science Foundation.

In Detail

The recent revitalization of the notion that we have a shortage of scientists, mathematicians, and engineers originated largely with Peter House of the National Science Foundation, but it was repeated by many NSF officials, including its former director, Erich Bloch. House projected shortages in 1985 and made his projections widely known. When the predicted shortages failed to materialize, people began to ask House difficult questions. Finally, at a legislative hearing, Senator David Boren got House to admit that his projections had been based on assumptions that bore no relationship to reality.

While House's shortages were failing to materialize, a certain type of article began to make its appearance with some regularity. One in *Newsweek* was headlined "No Ph.D.'s Need Apply" (Begley 1994). Four years earlier, a *New York Times* article was headlined "Amid 'Shortage,' Young Physicists See Few Jobs." That article reported that 12 percent of new physicists in 1990 received no job offers, and another 50 percent received one and only one (Browne 1992). The next year the *Times* was back to report on how tough it was even for graduates of the California Institute of Technology, the nation's premier engineering school, to find work. Undergraduates were going to graduate school because there were no jobs. New Ph.D.s were doing postdoctoral work because there were no jobs. Others were becoming permanent faculty, but they could not secure the usual positions leading to tenure. In fact, they were—are—highly educated permanent temps. The head of the physics department at Amherst put the figure in context when he reported how many applicants had applied for the single vacancy in his department: 813 (Kilborn 1993, p. A1).

The end of the cold war has exacerbated the surplus of scientists and engineers. More than in other nations, a significant portion of all scientists and engineers in the country work for the military-industrial complex. While the Pentagon has successfully kept its budget from declining too much, thousands of scientists have been thrown into the job market afresh because of decreased defense needs.

The glut in engineering is often ascribed to the arrival of many foreign students, and it is true that 50 percent of doctorates in engineering go to immigrants. Although there is now an increasing trend for these engineering graduates to return home—they can't get jobs here—nearly half do remain (Carson, Huelskamp, and Woodall 1993, p. 278). It's an enormous brain-gain for the country, and the only ones who suffer as a result are some undergraduates who are forced to receive instruction from people whose mastery of English is not up to lecturing at the college level.

Someone once said, in reaction to the increasing numbers of foreign students, "American kids don't like science anymore." The numbers don't bear out the claim. The percentage of 22-year-olds who get bachelor's degrees in science or engineering has been steady since 1959 and actually rose for a time as computers became pervasive in the culture. The number of native-born students who received doctorates in science or engineering declined from 1970 to 1980, but then the trend reversed and the number of doctorates is nearing the record level established in 1970 (Carson et al. 1993, p. 278).

In 1995 science writer Daniel Greenberg commented that "the paucity of solutions to the Ph.D. glut is surely one of the wonders of the great American university system. The common wisdom in the ivy-covered realm is that the problem will correct itself when students wise up to the grim job situation and stop coming." It hasn't happened yet.

A critic could argue that aside from actual scientists, we need a citizenry that is more knowledgeable about science and mathematics in order to deal with complicated science problems that have major ramifications for society, such as handling toxic wastes and ecology problems in general. That is probably true. In response, you could point to the increasing numbers of students taking science and mathematics courses, most of whom will be professionals in neither field. In addition, science courses and instruction are changing to incorporate more societal issues. The high school chemistry program Chemcom, for instance, begins with a social problem—a fish kill—and adds chemistry knowledge as needed. In Scotland, new courses simply called "technology" have been developed. Whereas pure science deals with understanding and involves problems that have right answers, technology challenges students with design problems that do not necessarily have a "best" answer. For instance, students might study issues involved in building a bridge across a river. A number of designs are possible, each with associated pros and cons.

In Sum

When someone worries out loud that we will soon be experiencing a shortage of scientists, engineers, and mathematicians, you can point to the articles cited in this section showing that we have a glut of people in all three professions. The widely disseminated reports of projected shortages were not based on realistic assumptions but were a ploy to generate more money for the National Science Foundation. Many students who receive bachelor's degrees in these fields go on to attain master's degrees, doctorates, and postdocs because they cannot find good work. A number of them become what have been called "permanent temps"—teaching at universities but not able to find a tenure-track position.

No evidence supports the oft-heard statement that the (nonexistent) shortage reflects the fact that "American kids don't like science anymore." The number of science courses taken in high school has been rising over the last 20 years. And the number of degrees awarded to native-born Americans in mathematics, science, and engineering has been rising for more than a decade. This has happened in spite of the fact that the number of high school graduates available to major in these fields declined virtually every year from 1977 to 1994.

It *is* true that U.S. graduates in these areas have been facing increasing competition from foreigners, especially in engineering. Currently, immigrants account for about 50 percent of all engineering Ph.D.s in the United States. On the other hand, about half of these stay on in this country, providing a tremendous brain-gain.

References

Begley, S. (December 6, 1994). "No Ph.D.'s Need Apply." *Newsweek*, pp. 62–63.

Browne, M.W. (March 10, 1992). "Amid 'Shortage' Young Ph.D.'s See Few Jobs." *New York Times*, p. C1.

Carson, C.C., R. M. Huelskamp, and J.D. Woodall. (May/June 1993). "Perspectives on Education in America." *Journal of Educational Research* 86, 5: 259–310.

Greenberg, D.S. (December 6, 1995). "Surplus in Science." *Washington Post*, p. A25.

Kilborn, P. T. (July 18, 1993). "Ph.D.'s Are Here But the Lab Isn't Hiring." *New York Times*, p. A1.

The Administrative Blob

What do I say when someone says, "School productivity is being smothered by an administrative blob"?

Few of the myths concerning schools can be so directly linked to one person as this one. The administrative blob is the creation of the overactive imagination of former Secretary of Education William Bennett.

In Brief

In brief, you can say the following: Schools are lean, though not mean.

In Detail

Central office staff account for 1.6 percent of the staffing in school districts. If we fired them all, teachers could get a 5 percent salary increase and class size could be reduced by one student (Robinson and Brandon 1992, p. 14). It's hard to see how those changes would increase productivity much.

Actually, people who make the comment about productivity are probably buying into a common but misbegotten metaphor of the school: the factory. This metaphor has afflicted schools since they became obsessed with Frederick Taylor's notions of "scientific management" in the second decade of this century. The disastrous aspects of the factory metaphor are considered in more detail in Chapter 15.

Figure 14.1 shows the spending pattern for one district—Aldine, Texas, just outside of Houston. I picked Aldine for no better reason than I happened to visit the district in 1996 and was given an annual report that contains the graph. The figures are prepared not by the district, but by the Texas Education Agency for all districts. Note that in this 44,000-pupil district, very little of the per-pupil expenditures go for either central or school (campus) administration.

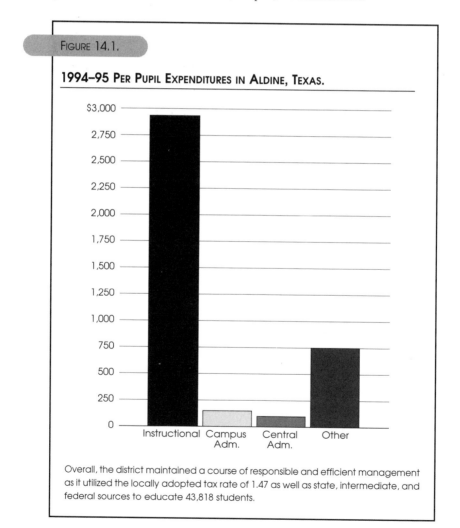

Figure 14.1.

1994–95 Per Pupil Expenditures in Aldine, Texas.

Overall, the district maintained a course of responsible and efficient management as it utilized the locally adopted tax rate of 1.47 as well as state, intermediate, and federal sources to educate 43,818 students.

Figure 14.2 presents the blob from a different perspective. From this graph we can see that if an administrative blob exists in schools, an administrative mountain exists in most other sectors of industry. For all sectors of industry, there are, on average, 7 frontline employees for every administrator (Robinson and Brandon 1992). Schools have almost 15.

In Sum

When someone says that huge numbers of bureaucrats are interfering with the schools' productivity, you can show them Figure 14.2 and say that "compared with nine other sectors of the economy, schools have a much lower ratio of supervisory employees to non-supervisory employees." Compared with all of the companies that are busy "downsizing," schools are already lean. In fact, the number of principals dropped from 118,000 in 1960 to 82,000 in 1993. In the same period of time, school enrollment climbed from 41,000,000 to 48,800,000 (National Center for Education Statistics 1994, p. 12). Staff

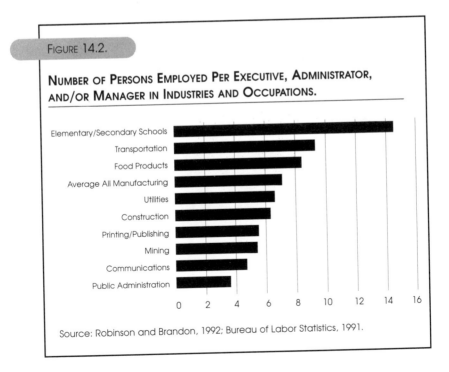

FIGURE 14.2.

NUMBER OF PERSONS EMPLOYED PER EXECUTIVE, ADMINISTRATOR, AND/OR MANAGER IN INDUSTRIES AND OCCUPATIONS.

Source: Robinson and Brandon, 1992; Bureau of Labor Statistics, 1991.

support positions, of course, have shown enormous growth, as schools have struggled to cope with state and federal mandates.

References

National Center for Education Statistics. (1994). *Digest of Education Statistics, 1994.* Washington, D.C.: Author.

Robinson, G., and D. Brandon. (1992). *Perceptions About American Education: Are They Based on Facts?* Arlington, Va.: Educational Research Service.

Teacher Accountability

What do I say when someone says, "Teachers should be accountable for their students' test scores"?

On its face, this is the most reasonable thing that has been said to us in this book. Of course teachers should be held accountable for kids' test scores. How else are we to evaluate their teaching? Behind this reasonable-sounding statement, however, lurks a vicious and untenable metaphor: the factory.

In Brief

In brief you can say the following:

- Test scores may well not reflect what was taught.
- Many things outside of school greatly affect test scores.
- Children are not raw material.
- The Law of WYTIWYG must be taken into account.

It is hard, I grant, not to sound defensive in saying any of these things, so often has the factory metaphor been hurled at—and accepted by—educators. But all four of the above statements are true.

In Detail

Concerning the first response, tests measure only a limited part of any curriculum area in a particular way. Pedagogically sound educational reforms might well not be detected by, say, the 40-item vocabulary test on the Iowa Tests of Basic Skills. For instance, the Key School, a public school in Indianapolis, is organized largely around the theory of multiple intelligences developed by Howard Gardner at Harvard. In attempting to develop all seven of the intelligences proposed by Gardner, students get not only the standard curriculum, but daily lessons in Spanish, in playing an instrument, and in art. They use computers frequently. Teachers also teach short courses in things that interest them outside of school—for example, pottery making and Victorian architecture.

The Key School has drawn praise from all quarters, but its test scores haven't moved much, if at all. And why should they? Indeed, the specialized vocabularies that the children will pick up studying Victorian architecture or music are most unlikely to turn up on vocabulary tests simply because they *are* specialized words. It is possible that these words might turn up on the SAT, and it is possible that learning Spanish might result in a student figuring out the Latinate root of an otherwise obscure SAT word, but these are long-term outcomes only tangentially related to the overall program of the school.

Concerning the second response, Glen Robinson and David Brandon (1994) of the Educational Research Service found that they could account for 83 percent of the variability in NAEP test scores among states with just four variables: parental education, number of parents in the home, type of community, and state poverty levels for ages 5–17. William Cooley (1993) at the University of Pittsburgh reached similar conclusions for the districts of Pennsylvania. Certainly some people will be quick to observe that none of those powerful variables are under the control of teachers.

Why do people want to ignore this evidence? Partly, I think, because people often need a scapegoat and schools are quite handy. But back in the 1960s, in the early days of "The Coleman Report," people were wondering if school mattered at all. "It's all family" was the early and simplistic interpretation of that study (see

Chapter 9). Schools do matter, but variables associated with family matter more.

The third response refers to the factory model of schools, which is insidious because human beings are not, either at birth or at any time in their lives, "raw material." Businesspeople are very fond of the factory metaphor, but I imagine if you went up to one and said, "Your daughter sure is fine raw material," you'd be lucky to escape without having a fist aimed at your face. Businesspeople recognize their own children as individuals, but when they get to thinking about children in general, they start using poor abstractions. They forget that kids have minds of their own, that they will love you, hate you, make you laugh and cry, lie to you, seek you out for comfort. Raw material doesn't do that. We would do better to try and convince people that a gardening metaphor is more appropriate. With nourishment, children grow into learned adults. Indeed, we acknowledge this metaphor at the beginning of school: *kindergarten* is German for "garden of children."

You can also say that not only is the raw material of a factory passive, the factory can specify its qualities. Schools—at least public schools—have no means of asserting "quality control."

As noted in connection with the Key School, tests (at least commercial achievement tests) cannot reflect any kind of tailored curriculum. A test-maker wants to sell tests all across the nation. To do so, the test-maker must examine the most commonly used textbooks and related materials and choose from them the material that appears most frequently.

Well, if we cannot hold teachers accountable for the level of test scores, can we hold them accountable for changes in test scores? Possibly. First, we have to know for certain that the material on the test reflects what is being taught in the classroom. Then it would make sense to give a test at the beginning of the year and again at the end to see how much had been learned. Indeed, the concept of a "criterion referenced test" originally included the idea of progress over time referenced to clearly stated benchmarks. Again, however, commercial tests do not lend themselves to such comparisons, in part because they are not attuned to specific curriculums.

The fourth response, the listing of the law of WYTIWYG—What You Test Is What You Get—is included merely to remind people that if teachers *are* held accountable for test scores, teachers can be expected to spend more time on material that the test covers. This requires, at the very least, that people be careful about what they test for. Some years ago, John Murphy became superintendent of the Prince George's County public schools in Maryland. Among other things, Murphy promised to raise test scores and to close the gap in scores between black and white students. Murphy turned one room in the administration offices into the "applied anxiety room," with the test score trends of all of the county's schools posted on the walls. Test scores began to rise, and they rose faster for black students than for white.

But strange stories began to emanate from Prince George's indicating that a lot of instruction in the county looked like preparation for the California Achievement Test (CAT). Students would go to the board and, as on the CAT, choose an answer from among four or five offered. Several organizations proposed evaluations of the reforms. Murphy steadfastly refused. Scores continued to rise.

Like all states, however, Maryland eventually adopted a new test for the state program. As usually happens, scores all over the state fell. But those in Prince George's County plummeted. Black students whose scores had risen well above the national norm of the 50th percentile on the CAT found themselves scoring as low as the 18th percentile on the new test. The ethnic gap yawned as wide as ever. Fortunately for Murphy, he had taken a job in another state.

In Sum

When someone says teachers ought to be held accountable for their pupils' test scores, you can say that you agree, but only if certain conditions are met: (1) the accountability must factor in what the child brings to the classroom (John Locke notwithstanding, no child is a *tabula rasa*); (2) the test must reflect what is being taught in the classroom; (3) the focus must be on *changes* in test scores, not *levels* of test scores (the level of achievement is powerfully affected by family and community variables not under the school's control); and (4) the test must not narrow the curriculum.

References

Cooley, W.W. (Summer 1993). "The Difficulty of the Educational Task: Implications for Comparing Student Achievement in States, School Districts, and Schools." *ERS Spectrum* 11, 3: 27–31.

Robinson, G.E., and D.P. Brandon. (1994). "NAEP Test Scores: Should They Be Used to Compare and Rank State Educational Quality?" Stock No. 0182. Arlington, Va.: Educational Research Service.

Dumb Teachers

What do I say when someone says, "Students who go into teaching are dumber than those who go into other fields"?

This is a myth that derives from a single fact: high school seniors who say they intend to major in education have lower SAT and ACT scores than do those who say they have other intended majors. Of course, most students don't declare a major until the end of their sophomore year in college and some change majors more than once.

In Brief

In brief, you can say the following:

• SAT scores are lower for education majors because education majors are overwhelmingly women, and women get lower SAT scores than men. Although studies show that women—no matter what their intended major—average about 45 points lower on the SAT-M than men do, women get higher grades in all levels of freshman college math, from remedial to advanced. One study found that before taking any courses in education, potential teachers had the same college grade point average as those in other fields.

In Detail

After *A Nation at Risk* appeared in 1983, it was fashionable among the political appointees (as opposed to career civil servants) in the U.S. Department of Education to blame teachers for the crisis. Teachers, some people contended, just weren't very bright (this was not a new allegation. In the years following Sputnik's launch in 1957, curriculum makers attempted to design "teacher proof" materials to protect them from the inept hands of teachers). Some people also feared that the women's movement and civil rights movement had had a detrimental impact on teaching. People for whom teaching had historically been one of the few good occupations available now had other options. The Department's Office of Planning, Budget, and Evaluation commissioned a study to document this widely "known" fact.

But the study found teachers no different from anyone else (Lee 1984). The study looked at various grade points of potential teachers and those who, in college, intended to major in a subject area. "Potential teachers" were defined as those who, in their freshman college year, said that they intended to major in education or said they intended to major in some other subject and then teach.

In high school, there was virtually no difference in grade point averages between potential teachers and those intending to major in arts and humanities, sciences, or business administration. In college, grade point differences between the two groups were nonexistent. At the end of their sophomore year, potential teachers had attained a GPA of 2.88, while those who did not plan to teach had a GPA of 2.87. Note that at the end of their sophomore year, the potential teachers would not have taken any of the reputedly easy courses in a school of education. At the end of their senior year, potential teachers had a GPA of 3.05, while the GPA of those in other fields reached 2.95. This doesn't smack of rampant grade inflation in education courses.

Confronted with this result, said Lee in a telephone conversation, the Department lost interest and the study was never published. "We made a presentation to the Department," said Lee. "It didn't go over well with the political appointees." Program Officer Dan Morrisey did put the research in the ERIC system, however.

Even ignoring the male-female SAT differential, it is not surprising that would-be teachers score lower on the SAT. People who score high on tests of all kinds are encouraged to go into higher-paying, more prestigious jobs. Given the abuse that schools have taken in the last 50 years, it is amazing that we can find enough teachers to fill the positions available. In an era in which many bright young graduates are looking at six-figure salaries not long after graduation, teachers are averaging $37,000 a year. And they're earning that much on average only because we have a very experienced teaching force. New hires are still coming into schools for $22,000 to $25,000 a year. Even so, 10 percent of those intending to major in education are among the top 20 percent of all SAT scorers (Berliner and Biddle 1995).

Beyond that, one can observe that the SAT is not a reliable predictor of job success for any profession and that it predicts even less well for teachers (Berliner and Biddle 1995). When one thinks about the nature of teaching, this is not surprising. The SAT is limited to a narrow band of verbal and quantitative skills. Teachers need a lot of social skills to deal with the varying personalities of the students that they are in contact with all day. They also must have a strong sense of autonomy, since they interact with other adults very little during the school day.

One can also note that teaching, in contrast to many other professions, takes place in a highly public arena where many other adults can render judgments on performance. This is not true for many other professions. As Berliner and Biddle (1995) point out, the third-leading cause of preventable death in this country each year is medical malpractice, with about 80,000 people dying from medical incompetence—twice as many as in automobile accidents. Only smoking and alcohol take a higher toll. One wonders how the public would judge the competence of doctors, and other professionals, if they wiped out 80,000 people a year on the same public stage as that on which teachers work.

In any case, every public school teacher has a college degree, and 70 percent of their coursework was taken outside the school of education. Fifty percent have master's degrees. In the United States, only about 25 percent of the population have even a bachelor's degree.

In Sum

When someone casts aspersions on teachers' abilities, tell them to stop looking at high school SAT scores. The notion that teachers are dumber than other college majors comes from what high school seniors tell ETS their major will be in college. Those who intend to major in education have lower SAT scores than students declaring most (but not all) other intended majors. But this is because women have lower SAT scores than men, and women account for most of those saying they might major in education.

A number of research studies have shown women to have lower SAT scores than men but to earn higher grades in college. In one study of 44,000 students that looked at all levels of freshman mathematics courses, the women averaged 45 points lower than men on the SAT, but earned slightly better grades.

You can also say that one study looked at the grades of various majors in their first two years of college—to wit, the years before education majors begin to take the supposedly easy, grade-inflated education courses. Education majors did not get lower grades than other majors.

You can also mention that, nationally, about 25 percent of the population over age 25 have a college degree, whereas 100 percent of all public school teachers have at least a bachelor's degree.

References

Berliner, D.C., and B.J. Biddle. (1995). *The Manufactured Crisis: Myths, Fraud, and the Attack on America's Public Schools.* New York: Addison Wesley.

Lee, John B. (October 25, 1984). "Tomorrow's Teachers" ERIC Document No. ED 263 042.

"Feel Good" Education

What do I say when someone says, "Educators are spending too much time teaching kids to feel good about themselves and not enough time teaching academics"?

This is a common theme these days. Some critics like to cite the work of Harold Stevenson, which purportedly shows that kids in the United States feel good about their mathematics ability but score low on math tests, whereas Asian kids feel bad about their mathematics ability but score high. This is not what the fatally flawed research actually showed, but this is the oft-heard interpretation.[1] This misinterpretation is taken as evidence that schools are emphasizing feeling good over high achievement.

In a related vein, critics of outcomes-based education claimed that it changed the three Rs into what Phyllis Schlafly called the three Ds: Deliberately Dumbed Down. If you are going to teach all kids the same thing, the argument went, you are not going to teach any

---

[1] Several observers have noted that an equally plausible interpretation focuses on Asian kids and their aversion to self-promotion. As someone who has lived in Asia, I can corroborate this observation: Asians simply don't brag about anything. If an Asian says to you, "I think you may find an acceptable meal in this restaurant," you have just received a five-star recommendation for the restaurant.

of them very much. If an outcome is to have all children dunk a basketball through the hoop, the hoop cannot remain 10 feet above the ground. This dumbing down was seen as an attempt to preserve the self-esteem of low-ability students.

In some quarters, the emphasis on self-esteem has been taken as simply part of a general war on excellence. Honor rolls, valedictorians, and many other forms of scholarship recognition have disappeared in a misguided attempt to keep low-ability kids from feeling bad. In the chapter entitled "The Attack on Excellence" in his book *Dumbing Down Our Kids,* Charles Sykes expressed the critique in a fairly typical way:

> The sculptured blond quarterback and prom queen have been awarded accolades by nature that cannot easily be repealed. Try as they might, the legions of therapists, social workers, and educationists will not be able to level these advantages or sooth the wounded self-esteem of the dorky, the homely, and the flat-chested. So they focus instead on the academic achievers: the handful of students who have ability and have worked hard enough to excel in their school work (1995, p. 68).

Sykes's commentary is presented simply because it is typical. The reader is left to consider the many implicit and untested assumptions in his statement. It should be noted that Sykes provides many anecdotes but no hard evidence. And if his recounting of my first "Bracey Report" is any indication, he is perfectly willing to alter facts to make his argument. He claims that I wrote the first report while acting as an "ideologist" for the National Education Association (NEA). In fact, the article was written while I was Director of Research and Evaluation for the Cherry Creek (Colorado) Schools, months before I took a job as a policy analyst at the NEA, a fact clearly noted in the credit line of the essay.

In Brief

In brief, you can say the following:

• No data exist to show how much time is being spent on building self-esteem.

- Some really dumb things have been done in schools in the name of self-esteem.
- Self-esteem is a very complicated concept—more than 200 instruments measure it, and they don't all measure the same thing.
- The critics of self-esteem often have an implicit, and false, assumption that learning is necessarily a bitter pill to swallow.
- The critics of self-esteem often have an implicit, and false, assumption that happy children will not learn.
- Many activities in school can promote both achievement and self-esteem.

In Detail

Because we have no data that directly bear on the topic, the following is a general discussion of self-esteem and its discontents. And we must note at the outset, as indicated in a couple of the "in brief" comments, a discussion of self-esteem often involves leaving the realm of data and entering the realm of long-held, intensely felt conceptions of what motivates people, how the world works, and what the proper values of our culture ought to be. The best summary of how these assumptions and values interact is likely that found in Alfie Kohn's "The Truth About Self-Esteem" (1994).

First off, it must be admitted that the whole field of self-esteem, and especially improvement of self-esteem, is confused and rife for caricature. Such caricatures became common after 1989, when a publicly funded task force was appointed in California to study the topic and it implications. To many, the idea of a self-esteem task force was the kind of flaky idea that could be taken seriously only in flaky California. The work of the task force was satirized in comic strips such as "Doonesbury" and "Calvin and Hobbes." The smirks increased when the task force, after reviewing massive amounts of research, came to this conclusion:

> The associations between self-esteem and its expected consequences are mixed, insignificant, or absent. The nonrelationship holds between self-esteem and teenage pregnancy, self-esteem and child abuse, self-esteem and most cases of alcohol

abuse and drug abuse. . . . If the association between self-esteem and behavior is so often reported to be weak, even less can be said for the causal relationship between the two. Over the years, other reviewers have offered fairly similar readings of the available research, pointing to results that are unimpressive, or characterized by massive inconsistencies and contradictions (Smelser 1989, p. 15).

The hope of the commission was to show that high self-esteem would act as what it referred to as a "social vaccine," enhancing prosocial behavior and reducing antisocial behavior. However, some studies found that joining gangs and engaging in a variety of delinquent behaviors enhanced self-esteem.

Some self-esteem programs in schools clearly seem misguided and hollow. It likely does little good to have children looking at bulletin boards that say "You are beautiful," or filling in forms completing the statement "I am special because," or having their teachers declare "You can do anything." Indeed, these statements are often contradicted by posted rules made up by adults and by rewards and punishments that demean the children and subvert the program. The school that had all of the above also had children hold their hands over their mouths when they returned from recess and physically isolated children who talked out of turn. In addition, it is unlikely that such exercises in feeling good as those mentioned above would carry much weight against the events in the child's family. I am reminded of Duke Ellington's comment that he was so loved he was two years old before his feet touched the earth.

Worse to some observers, and here we enter the realm of philosophy as well as child development, such self-esteem programs emphasize "me" at the expense of "us." Is it wise, they wonder, to concentrate on the individual self and risk increasing self-absorption rather than to emphasize community? They point out that the term *self-esteem* was popularized by Nathaniel Branden, an ardent disciple of the hyper-individualistic philosophy of Ayn Rand. While the "me" generation and its descendants have provoked much discussion, little data are available that directly assess any change in communal activities. One book, *Bowling Alone*, did assert that people were participating less in social activities (Putnam 1995). However, the author did not actually collect data, but extrapolated from earlier trends. When *Newsweek* and *Washington Post* columnist Robert J. Samuelson (1996) actually looked at some figures, he found that most kinds of social gatherings were actually on the increase.

As noted above, most observers agree that the environment of the child is a much more powerful force in his or her development than are self-esteem exercises. Also, if the school limits its efforts to such attempts it might be legitimating a cruel status quo. A child who is being abused is unlikely to have his ego fixed by saying "I am special," and if the school does nothing more, it endorses the child's status quo at home.

Many criticisms of self-esteem programs contain implicit theories of learning and development. As Kohn (1994) notes,

> They make the following argument: if students are expected to work hard, if they are graded strictly and rewarded or praised only when they have earned it, they will come to develop a sense of self-respect, which is (depending on the critic) either better than self-esteem or a prerequisite for it. In contrast, frequent praise will lead to vulgar self-satisfaction. This, in turn, discourages students from working hard (p. 278).

The above description is readily recognized as one form of various traditional approaches to schooling. It has a long history. When Ralph Tyler (1976) reflected on his experiences in school in the second decade of this century, he recalled that "[t]he view held by most teachers and parents was that the school's tasks should be sufficiently distasteful to the pupils to require strong discipline to undertake them and carry them through." There is little data to buttress this position (just as there is not much to buttress programs of self-esteem). It is a somewhat plausible notion, but without much support in the research literature. It is often, though not necessarily, accompanied by the belief that failure is actually a good thing:

> Once upon a time you passed or you failed. You made the team or you didn't. If you fell short, if your ego was bruised by get-

ting a D or by seeing your name on the cut list, then you buck-
led down and you made it the next time and felt good about
yourself. . . . Failure can be a terrific motivator (Powers 1993).

Anecdotes such as this one abound and, no doubt, in some
instances, failure is a motivator. There is, alas, no way of knowing
for any individual child whether it will motivate or demoralize. The
research data do not support motivation.

Related to the specific attacks on self-esteem are contentions that
schools should focus on academics to the exclusion of all affective
concerns. This, of course, is impossible in the school context and
silly as well. The study of literature, for instance, must involve discussion of morals, conflict, and values, as well as provide skills in the
careful use of language. Similarly, a study of science ought to indicate conflicts as one theory bumps up against another—Newton versus Einstein, evolution versus creationism, or Galileo versus the
Catholic Church. And in history, well, never mind.

Those who propose self-esteem programs have never made a
very strong case for the damaging outcomes of failure in part
because the impact of failure seems to be different in different areas.
Most students *don't* make athletic teams or orchestras and seem to
accept this with equanimity. Similarly, no stigma appears to be
attached to saying "I'm not good at math," but an enormous one is
attached to the inability to read. Indeed, being particularly good in
school subjects has always been suspect. One cannot rule out that
the demeaning of the academic is a defense mechanism protecting
the self-esteem of the mediocre, but the bulk of evidence in books
such as *Anti-Intellectualism in American Life* (Hofstedter 1962) suggests that it reflects a genuine distrust.

In Sum

There is no good, simple answer to assertions about self-esteem
programs. Such programs are probably much fewer in number than
the critics contend. The critics are prone to characterize them as "the
prevailing wisdom," or "the reigning orthodoxy," but as with so many
fads and reforms, most classrooms continue as they have in the past.

References

Hofstdeter, R. (1962). *Anti-Intellectualism in American Life.* New York: Alfred A. Knopf.

Kohn, A. (December 1994). "The Truth About Self-Esteem." *Phi Delta Kappan,* 76, 4: 272–283.

Powers, J. (January 24, 1993). "Feeling Good (for Nothing)." *Boston Globe,* p. 8.

Putnam, R. (1995). *Bowling Alone: The Decline of American Social Capital.* Cambridge, Mass.: Havard University Press.

Samuelson, R.J. (April 10, 1996). "*Bowling Alone* Is Bunk." *Washington Post* p. A19.

Smelser, N.M. (1989). "Self-Esteem and Social Problems." In *The Social Importance of Self-Esteem,* edited by A.M. Mecca. Berkeley, Calif: University of California Press.

Sykes, C. (1995). *Dumbing Down Our Kids: Why American Children Feel Good About Themselves But Can't Read, Write, or Add.* New York: St. Martin's Press.

Tyler, R. (1976). *Perspectives on American Education: Reflections from the Past, Challenges for the Future.* Chicago: SRA.

Special Education Costs

What do I say when someone says, "Schools are spending too much money on special education"?

This comment has been heard with increasing frequency in recent years as stories have surfaced reporting that districts have been found spending $50,000 or more a year on a single pupil.

In Brief

In brief, you can say the following:

- The amount of money spent on special education has been rising dramatically in the last 25 years.
- The question of whether or not this amount is too much cannot be settled with evidence. It is a matter of values. It is a matter of what a society owes its citizens and what they in return owe it. People will always disagree here.

In Detail

We saw in Chapter 3 that spending on schools rose 61 percent in real dollars in the last 25 years. We also saw that more than one-third of that money went directly into special education programs. Nationally, the average student receiving special education services costs a district 2.3 times as much per year as a regular student.

Nationally, about 12 percent of all students are receiving special education services, an increase from 10 percent in 1979 (National Center for Education Statistics 1994, p. 65).

Is this 2.3 multiplier too much? One position would say no, using a hospital analogy: hospitals are morally obligated to spend the most money on the most difficult patients. Schools should be, too. Another position would say yes, because children receiving special education services will not return to society nearly as much on the investment as will other children. People who hold this position often argue as well that highly able students should receive many more funds because they disproportionately return to society large benefits for the dollars invested in their education.

A third position, somewhat in between these two, contends that, indeed, the children needing special services should receive them, but that schools should not have to bear the burden. Why, they ask, should the taxpayers of the whole district be responsible for the exceptional education costs of a few?

And yet another position holds that what is good for special education students is good for all. Why should some students get special attention and others just get a "normal" education. All kids have some special needs. All kids deserve to be treated alike. All kids need an IEP (Individual Education Program) like those required by Public Law 94-142, which orders them for special education students.

As noted, this issue cannot be settled by evidence. Even if everyone agreed to a common measure of how much society benefits from students' education, and even if everyone agreed that the benefits returned to society from special needs children were not as large as those from others, that would not settle the issue. As framed in the last sentence, the issue is argued solely in economic terms, but perspectives other than the economic one may be used for deciding what is socially appropriate.

School budgets, however, are likely to become more strapped in the future than they are now, and special education costs are likely to continue to increase more rapidly than regular education costs. The fights among the groups contending for scarce dollars could become increasingly nasty.

192

In Sum

In sum, we see that the proportion of students receiving special education services has been increasing over time. It is, therefore, not surprising that the proportion of school expenditures going for special education has also increased, receiving over one third of all new money in the last 25 years. As noted in the body of the text, however, whether this amount is "too much" depends on assumptions about societal obligations that remove the question from the realm of solution by data.

Reference

National Center for Education Statistics. (1994). *Digest of Education Statistics, 1994.* Washington, D.C.: Author.

Epilogue

We have now considered 18 oft-repeated but erroneous myths concerning the nation's public schools. So where are we? Well, let's first consider where we are *not*. We are *not* in a position of saying "Things are fine, call off the reform." As I stated at the start of another book, you do not have to predicate reform on the assumption of failure. Even companies operating in the black sometimes find it a good thing to "re-engineer" the corporation.

The notion that reform is unneeded rests on a faulty assumption, a common one. The assumption is that the condition of education is like an on-off switch. If you are IBM CEO Louis V. Gerstner Jr., the switch is off, and you declare that "the system is broken." On the other hand, people in schools are too prone to think the switch is on, and therefore nothing needs to be done. But schools are not like an on-off switch. They are like the environment. You don't "fix" the environment. You attend to a species or to acid rain or to smog or to the disposal of hazardous waste. You attend to one problem at a time. New problems are always popping up because technological developments or even environmental advances in one sector have unanticipated consequences in another.

New problems are forever turning up in education as well. For instance, one study found that when teachers encounter children who are engaged with school, they act in a manner that reinforces the engagement (Skinner and Belmont 1992). So far, so good. That's a very human response. That's what teachers ought to do. But when they encounter children who are disengaged from school, they act in ways that reinforce the disengagement. This, too, is a very human response. A kid who has no interest in what the teacher is about is a real turnoff to a teacher. But it is not the appropriate response for

194

the situation. Ways need to be found to get this kid interested in something that the school has to offer. Recall that the *Money* survey cited in Chapter 9 did not find a student body eager to learn. Some evidence suggests that students are less engaged with school now than they were 20 years ago. Since the evidence is from college students, presumably the most engaged segment of the population, this appears to be a problem large enough for many of us to consider.

The data from the Third International Mathematics and Science Study (TIMSS) strongly suggest that textbooks need to be reworked and that teachers need to approach them differently. The mathematics curriculum presented in textbooks has been characterized as "a mile wide and an inch deep." This is an overstatement, no doubt constructed for the press conference where it was delivered, but it contains more than a germ of truth. TIMSS reveals that teachers often try to cover everything in the textbook.

Trying to teach the textbook from cover to cover is a bigger problem than just trying to do too much in too little time. Textbook publishers, naturally, design their textbooks to sell to a broad market. This approach sometimes results in no real "design" at all: the kitchen sink approach to textbook construction. The textbook publishers assume that teachers will select their preferred approach to teaching a subject, but the evidence from TIMSS suggests that teachers "select" it all, even when some of the topics selected don't mesh into a coherent approach.

One reason that teachers opt for this approach is that they have little time to think about what they are teaching. They teach 50 percent more hours a week than German teachers and an even higher percentage more than Japanese teachers. It might well be time to invoke the aphorism of the Bauhaus school of architecture: Less Is More. We might do better by our children if we taught them fewer things in more depth.

The case-study data from TIMSS show that Japanese and U.S. teachers approach the teaching of mathematics differently. Perhaps there are valuable lessons in the videotapes of teachers at work. The data also show that U.S. teachers are among the most educated and least *trained* in the world. They have high levels of formal education but lack the long apprenticeships offered by many other countries.

Can we at long last change teacher preparation programs to make them appropriate to the later tasks that teachers face?

An earlier study found that middle school science teachers, even those with strong science backgrounds, "rigged" experiments about half the time so that students could not help but get the correct answer. If science requires hypothesis testing (and it does), these students were not learning science. The other half the time the teachers simply provided the students with the answers. The researchers conducting the study did not criticize the teachers; they criticized a system that requires teachers to confront six classes of 25 to 30 students each day.

The list above could be expanded. We are not lacking for problems to solve. Serious problems. Tough problems. But solving problems is a rather more constructive activity than, say, commissioning research to prove that teachers aren't very bright, as discussed in Chapter 16. (What would the Department of Education appointees have done if that study had produced the results they had anticipated? What would they have done to improve the condition of teaching to attract more intelligent applicants? Would they have dared "throw money at the schools"?)

Where we are is at the top of a mountain of data that refutes the most common epithets hurled at public education. It is interesting to take note of the critics' reactions to these data. Initially, they tried to ignore them. It was hard to get any media attention for them. Isolated articles about my work and those of the other "contrarians" stood out against a steady drumbeat of failure. But as the number of contrarians grew and the numbers appeared to be more and more in our favor, the critics then tried to say that the numbers are irrelevant. We stood accused, by the very people who had grabbed and selected numbers wherever they could find them, of using "numerically driven" arguments. "There's more to it than just the numbers," said the critics. And so there is. In "The Third Bracey Report on the Condition of Public Education," I offered this definition of education:

> The formation of habits of judgment and the development of character, the elevation of standards, the facilitation of under-

standing, the development of taste and discrimination, the stim-
ulation of curiosity and wondering, the fostering of style and a
sense of beauty, the growth of a thirst for new ideas and
visions of the yet unknown (Goodlad 1992, p. 3).

On the development of the above qualities, the numbers are indeed
largely silent. But not once in any article or report critical of schools
have these qualities been examined or questioned in any way that
led to this assessment. The kinds of arguments that the critics have
made are those that are contained within the statements that open
each chapter of this book, and especially those presented at the
beginning of Chapter 7 on international comparisons. Those are all
numerically driven arguments. Having now lost, the critics want to
change the rules of the game.

The high school graduation rate in the United States has swelled
from 3 percent a century ago to 83 percent now. The history of
American education is a history that, save for the decade from 1965
to 1975, was a century of ever-increasing universality of secondary
education *and* progress in educational attainments. We cannot rest
on any laurels, but we can be proud of that record even as we seek
to improve it.

References

Goodlad, J. (November 1992). "Toward Educative Communities and
Tomorrow's Teachers." Works in Progress Series, No. 1. Seattle:
University of Washington.

Skinner, E., and M. Belmont. (December 1993). "Motivation in the
Classroom: Reciprocal Effects of Teacher Behavior and Student
Engagement Across the School Year." *Journal of Educational
Psychology* 85, 4: 571–581.

Figures

1.1   Expenditures for K–12 Education as a Percent of Per Capita Income in 16 Industrialized Nations (1985).   15

1.2   K–12 Per Pupil Expenditures in 16 Industrialized Nations (1988 Dollars).   16

1.3   School Spending as a Percent of Gross Domestic Product (1988).   17

1.4   Public Spending on Education as Percent of Per Capita Gross Domestic Product (1988).   18

3.1   Achievement Trends for Iowa, Grade 3–8, on ITBS Test C (Composite).   32

3.2   ITED Average Composite Scores for Iowa (1962–1990).   33

3.3   Achievement Trends for National Norming Samples, Grades 3–8, on ITBS Test C (Composite).   34

3.4   Average Yearly Changes in Median Percentile Rank During the 1980s for Well-Known Commercial Achievement Tests.   36

3.5   Index of Social Health of the United States (1970–1992).   37

3.6   Trends in Average Reading Proficiency for the United States as Measured by NAEP (1971–1992).   39

3.7   Trends in Average Mathematics Proficiency for the United States as Measured by NAEP (1973–1992).   40

3.8   Trends in Average Science Proficiency for the United States as Measured by NAEP (1969–70 to 1992).   41

4.1   SAT Subpopulation Scores (1975 and 1995).   50

4.2   How Low-But-Rising Scores Can Lower Averages.   51

4.3   The Great SAT Decline (1963–1991).   53

4.4   Average SAT (SAT Profiles, 1967–1990).   54

5.1   Trend Line for High-Scorers on SAT-V, 1941–1995.   60

5.2   Number (and Proportion) of Students Scoring Above
      650 on the SAT Verbal and Mathematics, According
      to *Education Week.*   63

5.3   Number (and Proportion) of Students Actually Scoring
      Above 650 on the SAT Verbal and Mathematics.   63

7.1   U.S. Ranks and Scores on IAEP-2, with International
      Averages.   79

7.2   Mathematics Proficiency Scores for 13-Year-Olds in
      Countries (1991) and Public 8th Grade Students in
      State (1992).   81

7.3   Combined IAEP-2 and NAEP Mathematics Proficiency
      Scores for Selected High-Achieving Student Groups.   83

7.4   Combined IAEP-2 and NAEP Mathematics Proficiency
      Scores for Selected Low-Achieving Student Groups.   84

7.5   7th Graders' Percentile Test Scores by Course Grades;
      Low- and High-Poverty Schools (1991).   86

7.6   8th Graders' Scores on Arithmetic Tests of the 1987
      Second International Mathematics Study.   87

7.7   8th Graders' Scores on Algebra Test of the 1987
      Second International Mathematics Study.   88

7.8   Achievement Scores, Second International Mathematics
      Study, Grouped According to Course Taken and
      Compared with Japanese Samples.   89

7.9   Algebra Achievement Scores, Second International
      Mathematics Study, for U.S. Pre-Algebra and Algebra
      Students and Top Quintile of Japanese Students.   90

7.10 U.S. Ranks and Scores in 1992 International Reading
      Study, *How in the World Do Students Read?,*
      Compared with Highest-Ranking Nations.   106

8.1   Event Dropout Rates for Grades 10–12, Ages 15–24,
      by Sex and Race-Ethnicity (1978–1993).   114

8.2   Percent of College Freshmen Reporting That They
      Engaged in Selected Academic Behaviors During
      Their Senior Year in High School (1987–1995).   115

8.3   Status Dropout Rates for Persons Aged 16–24, by
      Race-Ethnicity (1972–1993).   116

8.4   HSB and NELS:88 10th to 12th-Grade Cohort Dropout
      Rates, by Demographic Characteristics (1982–1992).   117

9.1   NAEP Results for Public and Private Schools.   120
9.2   Mathematics Achievement at Grade 12 by Level of
      Parental Education, Public and Private Schools.   122
11.1 10 Fastest-Growing Jobs in the United States
      (1990–2005).   158
11.2 10 Occupations with Largest Numbers of Jobs
      (1990–2005).   159
14.1 1994–95 Per Pupil Expenditures in Aldine, Texas.   172
14.2 Number of Persons Employed Per Executive,
      Administrator, and/or Manager in Industries and
      Occupations.   173

200

Appendix A

More Recent Figures on Spending

Figures released in mid-December 1996, as this book was going to press, indicate that U.S. spending on schools has changed little in recent years. "U.S. Is Big Education Spender in Global Study" reads the headline in the December 11, 1996, issue of *Education Week,* reporting highlights from the 1996 edition of *Education at a Glance—OECD Indicators.*[1] As noted in Chapter 1, it's true that the United States spends more on education than other countries if the measure is constant 1993 U.S. dollars *and* if one considers all levels of education—and it is all levels that the headline refers to. Consider that the United States spends twice the international average for college students.

According to the OECD report, the United States has climbed the spending ladder a bit. The new rankings show spending by elementary and secondary levels separately, and America's high ranking stems in part from the fact that the United States treats elementary and secondary schools similarly while few other countries spend much for elementary education. The United States finished second only to Switzerland in elementary spending with a per-pupil cost of $5,492. No other country spends as much as $5,000, and only five spend as much as $4,000 for the elementary years. At the secondary level, Austria and Switzerland spend more than the $6,541 spent by the United States, but five countries spend more than $6,000 and another four spend more than $5,000.

---

[1]*Education at a Glance—OECD Indicators* ($50) and *Education at a Glance—Analysis* ($10) are available from the Organization for Economic Cooperation and Development, 2001 L St., N.W., Suite 650, Washington, D.C. 20036. 1-800-456-6323. They are also on the World Wide Web at http://www.oecdwash.org.

Again, different measures yield different results, but the difference between elementary and secondary spending makes a difference in rankings. As a percentage of gross domestic product (GDP), the U.S. ranks 6th of 27 countries in spending on elementary schools, but only 13th in spending on secondary schools. If one takes either of these GDP figures as an index of how much of its wealth a nation is willing to invest in education, the United States remains an average spender.

As noted in Chapter 1, less of the money in a U.S. school budget reaches the classroom because the United States provides so many services in addition to classroom instruction. Of 22 countries ranked, only Denmark, Sweden, and the Czech Republic spend a smaller proportion of their budget on teacher salaries. Only Denmark spends a higher proportion on other salaries. As noted in Chapter 3, the increases in spending over the last 25 years have largely gone for special education and other services that other countries do not provide or provide in lesser amounts.

Index

Accountability, of teachers, 175–179
  test scores and, 176
"Achieve"
  created by NGA, 5–6
  stated goals of, 6
Achievement in schools
  level of vs. changes in, 23
  and poverty, effect of, 84–86, 86f
  related to money spent, 20–26
    meta-analysis of, 23
    and restriction of range, 24
  and school organization,
    125–127
Achievement tests, vs. NAEP, 38
ACT, vs. SAT, 21–22
"Administrative blob," 16
  lack of evidence for, 31,
    171–174, 172f–173f
Advanced mathematics, increased
  curriculum for, 62
Aldine, Texas, per–pupil
  expenditures in, 172, 172f
Alexander, Lamar, and Bob Dole
  speech, 2
Algebra, SIMS scores on, 87–88, 88f
"America 2000: Educate America
  Act," 9
  opposition, concerns of, 134
American Federation of Teachers,
  and *New York Times*
  advertisement, 1, 72
*America's Choice: High Skills or
  Low Wages!*, 155
  and criticism of schools, 152
APEC forum (1996), 154
Arithmetic, SIMS scores on, 87, 87f
Asian Pacific Economic
  Cooperation (APEC) forum
  (1996), 154

Asian students, and SAT math
  scores, 61–62
Australia, school choice in, 142–143
Autonomy, of charter schools,
  146–147
Averages, and low-but-rising scores,
  effect of, 49, 51f

Bennett, William
  and "administrative blob," 16
  lack of evidence for, 31,
    171–174, 172f–173f
  and Bob Dole speech, 2
  and SAT scores vs. state
    spending on schools, 20–22
Berliner, David, 1, 4
  and effects of television, 61
  on "High School and Beyond,"
    Chubb and Moe analysis of,
    126
  and spending in U.S. schools, 13
Biddle, Bruce, 1, 4
  on "High School and Beyond,"
    Chubb and Moe analysis of,
    126
Bilingual education, and
  immigrants, 72
Blacks, dropout rates for, 113
Brigham, Carl Campbell, on SAT,
  capabilities of, 44
British Columbia, school choice in,
  143
Budgets. *See* School budgets
Bullying, in Japanese schools, 92
Bureaucracy, in schools, 171–174,
  172f–173f
Bureaucratic involvement, and
  school choice programs, success
  of, 141

Bush, George
  education agenda of, 124
  and first Education Summit
    (1989), 8–9
  and media coverage of
    education, 105
Business Roundtable, and *New York
  Times* advertisement, 1, 76

The Candidate's Handbook, 1996
  criticism of schools in, 2
  and SAT math scores, 61–62
Catholic schools, vs. public schools,
  123
Central Park East, school choice
  program in, 141
Charter schools, 138, 140, 144–148
  arguments for/against, 139
  autonomy in, 146–147
  claims of success in, 145–146
  and education-driven choice
    initiative, 136
  failure, results of, 146–147
  parental involvement in, 147–148
  and school choice, 145
  selection processes in, 147–148
  theory of, 146
Chubb, John, and analysis of "High
  School and Beyond," 125–127,
  129
Cities, and dropout rates, increase
  in, 118
Clinton, Bill, and "America 2000," 9
Cohort dropout rates, 113, 116, 117*f*
Cold War, criticism of schools
  during, 7
Coleman, James, and analysis of
  "High School and Beyond,"
  122–123
College
  entrance exams for
    in Japan, 96–97, 100
    in U.S. *See* ACT, vs. SAT;
      SAT
  percent of U.S. students
    attending, 14, 18
College-bound curriculum,
  democratization of, 49

Commodification of American life,
  Peter Cookson on, 137
Comparisons, of education systems,
  U.S. vs. other countries. *See*
  International comparisons
Completion rate, of high school, 118
Conformity, in Japanese schools,
  92, 100
Constraints, in private and public
  schools, 130
Consumer price index (CPI), and
  education, inflation for, 29
Controlled choice, of schools, 138
Cookson, Peter
  and free-market theory, 137
  on "High School and Beyond,"
    Chubb and Moe analysis of,
    126
  and school choice programs,
    129–130, 142
CPI. *See* Consumer price index, and
  education, inflation for
Credibility, of test scores, 32–34
"Crisis in Education" (*Life*, March
  1958), 7–8
Crisis in the Classroom, and student
  knowledge, 69
Criticism, of schools
  by Bob Dole, 2
  in *The Candidate's Handbook,
    1996,* 2
  during Cold War, 7
  generated by *A Nation at Risk,*
    152
  by Louis V. Gerstner, 2
  in *New York Times,* 1
Cultural literacy, 66
Curriculum
  advanced mathematics, increase
    in, 62
  college-bound, democratization
    of, 49
  narrowing of, and standardized
    tests, 178
  post-1957, and declining test
    scores, 38
  tailored, and test scores, 176

"Decade of distraction"
and SAT score decline, 46–47
and test scores, 37–38
Demographics
of Iowa, and test scores, 31–32
of SAT takers, changes in,
43–44, 46
and test scores, changes in,
31–32
Direct instructional model, in
Japanese educational system, 96
Discipline, in schools, 5
Disengagement, of students,
113–115, 115*f*, 194–195
Dole, Bob
criticism of schools, 2
on school choice, 3
Doyle, Denis
on international comparisons,
76
on SAT math scores, 61–62
on spending vs. test scores, 28
Dropout rates, 112–118
cohort, 113, 116, 117*f*
differential reporting of,
112–113
event, 113–115, 114*f*
rising in cities, 118
status, 113, 115–116, 116*f*
Dropouts
psychological, 113–115, 115*f*
and second-chance schools, 138
"Dumbing down," in outcomes-
based education, 184–185

Economic Policy Institute, on
inflation in education, 29
Economy, U.S.
competitiveness of, 152–154, 160
and Federal Reserve Board, 154
impact of schools on, 153–154
Education at a Glance (1993), 15
Education at a Glance (1996), 201
Education-driven choice initiative,
135–136
and charter schools, 136
Education expenditures
and higher education, 18, 201

out-of-classroom, 16–19, 202
as percent of dollars per pupil,
14, 16*f*
as percent of gross domestic
product, 15, 17*f*, 202
as percent of per capita gross
domestic product, 15, 18*f*
as percent of per capita
income, 14, 15*f*
per pupil, in Aldine, Texas, 172,
172*f*
and special education
programs, 17–19, 30–31,
191–193
and test scores, 28–42
vs. achievement, 20–26
Education in States and Nations
(1993), 14
Education majors
grade point averages of, 181
SAT scores of, 180, 182
Education, parental. *See* Parental
education/income levels, for
private vs. public schools
Education Summits (1989, 1996),
8–10
Education Week, SAT scores,
erroneous reporting of, 62–64, 63*f*
Edutrain charter school, failure of,
146–147
The End of Work, 159–160
Ethnic groups, and SAT scores, 50*f*
Event dropout rates, 113–115, 114*f*
Expenditures, educational. *See*
Education expenditures
Exploding the Myths, 1
Factory metaphor, used for schools,
175, 177
Fantini, Mario, and education-
driven choice initiative, 135–136
Federal Reserve Board, and U.S.
economy, effect on, 154
"Feel Good" education, 184–189
*Final Exam: A Study of the
Perpetual Scrutiny of American
Education*
and *A Nation at Risk*, criticism
of, 40–41
and standards, 11–12

Finn, Chester E. Jr., 2
  on Catholic vs. public schools,
    124
  on international comparisons,
    80
  on spending vs. test scores, 28
  on student knowledge, 66, 71
First Education Summit (1989), 8–9
"Flat" test scores, lack of evidence
    for, 31, 32f–34f
Food, and school budgets, 17
Free-market theory
  and charter school failure,
    146–147
  and school choice, 134,
    136–137, 142
Friedman, Milton, on free-market
  theory, 134

Geography, student knowledge of,
  in 1943, 68
Geometry, and U.S. students,
  performance of, 102–103
George, Paul, and Japanese
  educational system, 95–98
Germany, reading scores in, 107
Gerstner, Louis V.
  criticism of schools, 2
  on international comparisons,
    76
  and spending in U.S. schools,
    13
  on spending vs. test scores, 28
Ginn, Sam, on job skills of
  graduates, 164
Glass, Ira, on psychological
  dropouts, 113–114
Glass, Sandra, on constraints, in
  private and public schools, 130
Global marketplace
  in A Nation at Risk, 151–152
  and schools, 151–161
"Goals 2000," 9
Golden Age of education,
  widespread belief in, 69–70
"The Good—and the Not So
  Good—News About American
  Schools," 4

Governance-driven choice initiative,
  138
Government control, of schools,
  138
Government-industrial complex, 163
Graduation rate, for high school,
  197
Graphing, of SAT scores, 43, 52,
  53f–54f
Gray, C. Boyden, on international
  comparisons, 76
Great Britain, school choice in, 144
Greenspan, Alan, effect on U.S.
  economy, 154

Hanushek, Eric
  on money vs. achievement, 20
    reanalyses of, 22–24
  on spending vs. test scores, 28
Henig, Jeffrey
  on charter schools, 145
  on "High School and Beyond,"
    Chubb and Moe analysis of,
    126
  on school choice programs,
    141–142
Heritage Foundation, and criticism
  of schools, 2
Herrnstein, Richard, and college-
  bound curriculum,
  democratization of, 49
Higher education. See College
High school
  completion rate, 118
  graduation rate, 197
"High Schools and Beyond" (HSB)
  Chubb and Moe analysis of,
    124–127
  and cohort dropout rates, 116,
    117f
  Coleman analysis of, 122–124
High-tech vs. low-tech jobs, in U.S.,
  157–159, 158f–159f
Hirsch, E.D., on cultural literacy, 66
Hispanics
  dropout rates for, 113, 118
History, student knowledge of, in
  1943, 68

Holland
  "pillarization" in, 143–144
  school choice in, 143–144
House, Peter, and scientist shortage
  projections, 168
Houston, Paul, 1
Howe, Harold II, 46. *See also* The
  Wirtz Panel
*How in the World Do Students
  Read?,* 67, 102, 105–107, 106*f*
  media coverage of, 105–106
HSB. *See* "High School and
  Beyond"

IAEP-2. *See* Second International
  Assessment of Educational
  Progress in Mathematics and
  Science
IBM, CEO of. *See* Gerstner, Louis V.
Immigrants
  and bilingual education, 72
  legal vs. illegal, 47
Income levels
  parental, for private vs. public
  schools, 121, 122*f*
  and status dropout rates, 115–116
Index of Social Health, and test
  scores, 35–57, 37*f*
Individual Education Program
  (IEP), and special education, 192
Inflation, for education, and
  consumer price index, 29
Institute for Innovation in Social
  Policy, and Index of Social
  Health, 35–37, 37*f*
Interest rates, low, and wages, 155
International comparisons, 75–110
  difficulties inherent in, 77–78
  and *New York Times*
    advertisement, 76
  ranks vs. scores, 77–80, 79*f*
  and variability, within/between
    nations, 80–83, 81*f*
International Institute for
  Management, and U.S. economy,
  competitiveness of, 152–153
Iowa, demographics of, and test
  scores, 31–32

Iowa test norms, and national
  norms, similarity between, 34–35
Iowa Tests of Basic Skills (ITBS),
  changes in
  1955–1992, 31, 32*f,* 34*f*
  1946 vs. 1947, 71
Iowa Tests of Education
  Development (ITED), changes in,
  1962–1990, 31, 33*f*
Ishizaka, Kazuo, on Japanese
  educational system, 98–99
ITBS. *See* Iowa Tests of Basic Skills
ITED. *See* Iowa Tests of
  Educational Development

Japanese educational system,
  92–101
  college entrance exams in,
    96–97, 100
  curriculum presented vs.
    attained in, 98–99
  direct instructional model in, 96
  and *juku,* 93, 95, 97, 99
  reform efforts in, 100–101
  and social/psychological
    development, 97–98
  visitors, best schools shown to,
    98
Japanese National Institute for
  Educational Research, 98
*The Japanese Secondary School:
  A Closer Look,* 95–98
Jobs
  glorification of, in U.S., 165
  loss of, due to technology,
    159–160
  low–tech vs. high–tech,
    157–158, 158*f*–159*f*
  projections through year 2005,
    158*f,* 158–159, 159*f*
  student, and effect on
    achievement, 95
Job training, and schools, 162–166
Juku, in Japanese educational
  system, 93, 95, 97, 99

Kemp, Evan J., on international
  comparisons, 76

The Key School (Indianapolis), and test scores, 176
Knowledge, of students. *See* Student knowledge
Kohn, Alfie, on self-esteem, 186
Kolderie, Ted, and charter schools, 136
Krauthammer, Charles, on international comparisons, 76

"Lake Wobegon effect," and test scores, 32–33
Lankford, Hamilton, on special education expenditures, 30
Law of WYTIWYG, 178
Life Adjustment Education (curriculum), 45
Life magazine (March 1958), and "Crisis in Education" article, 7–8
Low-income students, taking SAT, 44
Low-tech jobs, college graduates in, 164
Low-tech vs. high-tech jobs, in U.S., 157–159, 158*f*–159*f*

Magnet schools, 138
and policy-driven choice initiative, 137–138
as school improvement issue, 138
The Manufactured Crisis, 1, 4
and effects of television, 61
and "High School and Beyond," Chubb and Moe analysis of, 126
Market analysis, and schools. *See* Free-market theory
Marshall, Ray, on U.S. economy, 155
Mathematics
achievement in
measured by NAEP, 40, 40*f*
measured by TIMSS, 101
advanced, increased curriculum for, 62
increased test scores in, 35, 36*f*
instruction in, 91–92

scores
for high-achieving groups, 82–83, 83*f*
for low-achieving groups, 83–84, 84*f*
for 13-year-olds, 81*f*
SIMS scores on, 87*f*, 87–88, 88*f*–90*f*
and societal issues, in curriculum, 169
U.S.–Japan comparison, 88–91, 89*f*–90*f*
algebra scores and, 90*f*, 90–91
by courses taken, 89*f*, 89–90
U.S. ranks and scores, vs. international averages, 79*f*
Mathematics SAT
and Asian students, 61–62
high scorers on, 59–61
predictions for scores, 50–51
Measurement, and U.S. students, performance of, 102
Media coverage
of education, during Bush administration, 105
of *How in the World Do Students Read?*, 105–106
of SAT score changes, 47
of student knowledge, 66–67
of TIMSS data, 104–105
Meta-analysis, of achievement—money relationship, 23
Miles, Karen Hawley
on inflation in education, 29
and special education expenditures, 31
on spending vs. productivity, 30
Mill, John Stuart
and school choice, 133–134
and state schools, coercive possibilities in, 133–134
Milwaukee Public Schools (MPS), vs. choice schools, 127–129
Milwaukee, Wisconsin, school choice program in, 2–3, 127–129, 140
Minnesota, school choice program in, 140

Minority students, taking SAT, 44
Moe, Terry, and analysis of "High
   School and Beyond," 125–127,
   129
Molnar, Alex
   on free-market theory, 137
   on Milwaukee choice program,
   129
Money magazine, and private vs.
   public schools, 130
Money, spent on schools. *See*
   Education expenditures;
   Spending, in U.S. schools
MPS. *See* Milwaukee Public Schools
Murray, Charles, and college-bound
   curriculum, democratization of,
   49

NAEP. *See* National Assessment of
   Educational Progress
Nathan, Joe, and charter schools,
   136
National Alliance of Business, and
   New York Times advertisement, 1,
   76
National Assessment of Educational
   Progress (NAEP)
   data used in *A Nation at Risk*,
   38–41, 39*f*–41*f*
   and IAEP–2, data merged with,
   82–84, 83*f*–84*f*
   and mathematics, achievement
   in, 40, 40*f*
   and reading, achievement in,
   39, 39*f*
   and science, achievement in,
   39–40, 41*f*
   scores correlated with
   spending, 25
   scores for private vs. public
   schools, 120*f*, 120–121
   vs. achievement tests, 38
National Center for Education
   Statistics, 14
National Commission on Excellence
   in Education. See *A Nation at
   Risk*
National Education Goals Panel, 9

National Education Longitudinal
   Study (NELS:88), and cohort
   dropout rates, 116, 117*f*
National Governors Association
   (NGA)
   and "Achieve," 5–6
   and *New York Times*
   advertisement, 1, 76
National Science Foundation, and
   scientist shortage projections, 168
National test norms, 35
   and Iowa norms, similarity
   between, 34–35
A Nation at Risk, 8
   and *Final Exam: A Study of the
   Perpetual Scrutiny of
   American Education*,
   criticized in, 40–41
   and global marketplace, 151–152
   and SAT score decline, 53
   use of NAEP data, 38–41,
   39*f*–41*f*
NELS:88. *See* National Education
   Longitudinal Study
Net Services Index, and inflation in
   education, 29
"New Biology," 72
"New Math," 72
"New Physics," 72
New York Times, advertisement
   against public schools, 1, 76
   and consequential validity of
   IAEP-2, 105
NGA. *See* National Governors
   Association
Nostalgia, regarding education,
   69–70

OBE. *See* Outcomes-based
   education
Occupations
   loss of, due to technology,
   159–160
   in U.S.
      low-tech vs. high-tech,
      157–158, 158*f*–159*f*
      projections through year
      2005, 158*f*, 158–159, 159*f*

OECD. *See* Organization for Economic Cooperation and Development

The One Best System: A History of American Urban Education, and education-driven choice initiative, 135–136

On Further Examination, and SAT decline (1963), 46–47, 53

On Liberty, and school choice, 133–134

Organization
  of public school opposition, 2–3
  of schools, and achievement, 125–127

Organization for Economic Cooperation and Development (OECD), 14–15, 201

Outcomes-based education (OBE), 9
  criticism of, 134, 184–185

Out-of-classroom expenditures, in school budgets, 16–19, 202

Parental education/income levels, for private vs. public schools, 121, 122*f*

Parental participation
  in charter schools, 148
  in U.S. schools, 142

Parental school choice, 135–136
  based on proximity, 134

Participation, parental
  in charter schools, 148
  in U.S. schools, 142

"Ph.D. glut," 168–170

"Pillarization," in Holland, 143–144

Policy-driven choice initiative, 137–138

Politics, Markets and America's Schools, and analysis of "High School and Beyond," 124–127

Postsecondary options, and school choice, 138

Poverty, and achievement, effect on, 84–86, 86*f*

Powell, Arthur, and curriculum, variety of in U.S., 129

Preliminary SAT. *See* PSAT, stable norms of

Private schools
  constraints faced by, 130
  vs. public schools, 119–131
  Money magazine report on, 130
  parental education/income levels and, 121, 122*f*
  test scores in, 120*f,* 120–121

Privatization, of schools, 2. *See also* Charter schools; School choice

Productivity
  of U.S. work force, 153, 155–156
  vs. spending, in U.S. schools, 30

Proximity, parental choice based on, 134

PSAT, stable norms of, 48–49

Psychological development, in Japanese schools, 97–98

"Psychological dropouts," 113–115, 115*f,* 194–195

Public Law 94-142, and special education, 192

Public schools
  constraints faced by, 130
  organized opposition to, 2–3
  vs. Catholic schools, 123
  vs. private schools, 119–131
  Money magazine report on, 130
  parental education/income levels and, 121, 122*f*
  test scores in, 120*f,* 120–121

Public Schools of Choice, and education-driven choice initiative, 135–136

Public scrutiny, of schools, and choice programs, 142

Pupil school choice, 135–136

Purchasing Power Parity Index (PPPI), and per-pupil expenditures, 14

Ravitch, Diane, on student knowledge, 66, 71

"Raw material," children viewed as,
   in factory model, 177
Raywid, Mary Anne, and school
   choice initiatives, 135–138
Reading
   achievement in
      increased, 35, 36f, 71–72
      measured by NAEP, 39, 39f
      emphasis on, in U.S. schools,
         92
      increased test scores in, 35, 36f
      scores, in Germany, 107
Reagan, Ronald, education agenda
   of, 122–124
Recentering, of SAT scores, 53–55
Recession, schools blamed for,
   152–153
Reinventing Education, 28
   and spending in U.S. schools,
      13
Religion, segregation by, in
   Holland, 143–144
Renorming, of SAT scores, 53–55
Restriction of range, and
   achievement—money
   relationship, 24
*Rethinking School Choice: Limits of
   the Market Metaphor,* 126
   and school choice, 141
Rifkin, Jeremy, and jobs lost to
   technology, 159–160
Rothstein, Richard
   on inflation in education, 29
   and special education
      expenditures, 31
   on spending vs. productivity, 30

Salaries, low, of teachers, 164, 182
Salisbury, Harrison, and Soviet
   Union, student knowledge about,
   68–69
The "Sandia Report," 1
   and SAT scores, 47, 52, 54f
   and special education
      expenditures, 30–31
SAT
   and "decade of distraction,"
      46–47

demographics of students
   taking, changes in, 43–44, 46
graphing of scores, 43, 52,
   53f–54f
history and development of,
   44–45
low-but-rising scores, effect on
   averages, 49, 51f
mathematics
   and Asian students, 61–62
   high scorers on, 59–61
   predictions for scores, 50–51
media coverage of, 47
"plummeting" scores on, 43–56
scores
   decline in (1963), 46–47, 53
   of education majors, 180, 182
   erroneous reporting of,
      62–64, 63f
   by ethnic group, 50f
   as supplementary record, 44–45
   and teaching success, non-
      predictor of, 182
verbal
   high scorers on, 59–61, 60f
   predictions for scores, 52
   score decline (pre-1951),
      45–46
vs. ACT, 21–22
Schneider, Joe, 1
School budgets
   and food, 17
   and out-of-classroom
      expenditures, 16–19, 202
   and special education
      programs, 17–19
   and transportation, 16–17
School choice
   arguments for/against, 139
   in Australia, 142–143
   Bob Dole speech on, 3
   in British Columbia, 143
   Central Park East (New York),
      program in, 141
   and charter schools, 144–148
   different types of, 138
   and free-market theory, 134,
      136–137

School choice (cont'd)
in Great Britain, 144
in Holland, 143–144
initiatives of, 135–138
Milwaukee, Wisconsin, program
in, 2–3, 127–129, 140
Minnesota, program in, 140
parental, 135–136
based on proximity, 134
and public scrutiny of schools,
142
pupil, 135–136
as "self-contained" reform, 125
success of programs, and
bureaucratic involvement, 141
as tool vs. as solution, 142
School Choice, 126
School organization, and
achievmement, 125–127
Schools
blamed for recession, 152–153
criticism of
by Bob Dole, 2
in *The Candidate's
Handbook, 1996,* 2
during Cold War, 7
by Louis V. Gerstner, 2
in *New York Times,* 1
discipline in, 5
factory metaphor used for, 175
job training and, 162–166
School systems, comparing across
nations. *See* International
comparisons
Science
achievement in
measured by NAEP, 39–40,
41*f*
measured by TIMSS, 101
instruction in, 91, 196
and societal issues, in
curriculum, 169
U.S. ranks and scores, vs.
international averages, 79*f*
Scientists
actual surplus of, 168–169
projected shortages of, 167–170
Scores. *See* Test scores

Second-chance schools, 138
Second Education Summit (1996),
10
Second International Assessment of
Educational Progress in Mathematics and Science (IAEP-2),
66–67, 79*f,* 81*f,* 102, 105
and NAEP data, 82–84, 83*f*–84*f*
Second International Mathematics
Study (SIMS), 87–88, 88*f*–90*f,*
101–103
Segregation by religion, in Holland,
143–144
Selection processes, in charter
schools, 147–148
Selective media coverage
during Bush administration, 105
of *How in the World Do
Students Read?,* 105–106
of SAT score changes, 47
of student knowledge, 66–67
of TIMSS data, 104
Self-esteem, school programs in,
184–189
Shanker, Albert, on international
comparisons, 75–76
The Shopping Mall High School, 129
Silberman, Charles, and student
knowledge, 69
Social development, in Japanese
schools, 97–98
Social health, index of, and test
scores, 35–57, 37*f*
Societal issues, in math/science, in
curriculum, 169
South Korean educational system,
93–94
Soviet Union, student knowledge
about, 68–69
Special education programs
increased spending for, 30–31,
191–193
and school budgets, 17–19
Spending, in U.S. schools, 13. *See
also* Education expenditures
formulas for computing, 14–18,
15*f*–18*f*
and higher education, 18, 201

Spending, in U.S. schools (cont'd)
vs. achievement, 20–26
vs. productivity, 30
Spillane, Robert R., on international
comparisons, 80
Standards
developed by professional
organizations, 10
issues surrounding, 5–12
Status dropout rates, 113, 115–116,
116f
income level and, 115–116
Stearns, Kathryn, and school
choice, in Great Britain, 144
Straight Talk About America's
Schools: Dispelling the Myths, 1
Student knowledge
about Soviet Union, 68–69
of history and geography, circa
1943, 68
past vs. current, 70
perceived decline in, 66–67
Ravitch and Finn study on, 71
selective reporting and, 66–67
Subsidization, of private schools,
142–143. See also School choice

Teacher accountability, 175–179
Teachers
future. See Education majors
low salaries of, 164, 182
training of, 195–196
Teaching, time spent, in U.S.
classrooms, 94–95
Technology, job loss due to,
159–160
Television, effects of, 61
Test norms, national vs. Iowa,
similarity between, 34–35
Test ranks, vs. scores, 77–80, 79f, 103
Test scores. See also specific tests
changes in, and demographics,
31–32
credibility of, 32–34
and curriculum, narrowing of,
178
and "decade of distraction,"
37–38

"flat," lack of evidence for, 31,
32f–34f
and Index of Social Health,
35–57, 37f
"Lake Wobegon effect" on,
32–33
non-school influences on, 176
and post-1957 curriculums, 38
in private vs. public schools,
120f, 120–121
and reading and math, gains in,
35, 36f
and tailored curriculum, 176
and teacher accountability, 176
and upper grades, declines in,
37–38
variability in, 80–83, 81f, 91
vs. ranks, 77–80, 79f, 103
Textbooks, reform of, 195
Thinking for a Living, 155
Third International Mathematics
and Science Study (TIMSS), 94,
101–102
case studies in, 104
curriculum analyses in, 104
media coverage of, 104–105
ranks vs. scores in, 103
and textbook reform, 195
The Thirteenth Man, and Golden
Age of education, 69–70
"Throwing money at schools,"
20–26
Training, of teachers, 195–196
Transportation, and school budgets,
16–17
"The Truth About Self-Esteem"
(1994), 186
Tucker, Marc, on U.S. economy, 155
Tyack, David, and education-driven
choice initiative, 135–136

Unemployment, 155
Upper grades, and test scores,
declines in, 37–38
Urban dropout rates, increase in, 118
U.S. Department of Education, and
New York Times advertisement, 1,
76

U.S. economy
    competitiveness of, 152–154, 160
    and Federal Reserve Board,
        effect of, 154
    impact of schools on, 153–154
U.S. work force
    produced by schools, 151–161
    productivity of, 153, 155–156, 160

Variability
    in scores
        U.S. vs. Japan, 91
        within/between nations, and
            international comparisons,
            80–83, 81f
Verbal SAT
    decline pre-1951, 45–46
    high scorers on, 59–61, 60f
    predictions for scores, 52

Wages, and low interest rates, 155
Walberg, Herbert .
    on Japanese education system, 92
    and spending in U.S. schools, 13
We Must Take Charge, 66
Westbury, Ian, and U.S.–Japan math
    comparison, 88–91, 89f–90f
What Do Our 17-Year-Olds Know?,
    66
What You Test Is What You Get
    (WYTIWYG) law, 178
Whittington, Dale, and student
    knowledge, 70

Will, George, on money vs.
    achievement, 21
The Wirtz Panel
    and PSAT norms, 48–49
    SAT decline (1963), report on,
        46–47, 53
Wirtz, Willard, 46. See also The
    Wirtz Panel
Witte, John
    and choice program, in
        Milwaukee, Wisconsin,
        127–129
    on "High School and Beyond,"
        Chubb and Moe analysis of,
        126–127
Women, taking SAT, 44
Work
    glorification of, in U.S., 165
    school preparation for, 162–166
Work force, U.S.
    produced by schools, 151–161
    productivity of, 153, 155–156,
        160
Working students, and effect on
    achievement, 95
World Economic Forum, and U.S.
    economy, competitiveness of,
    152–153
Wurtzel, Alan, and high school
    graduate, job skills of, 163
Wyckoff, James, on special
    education expenditures, 30
WYTIWYG, law of, 178

G erald W. Bracey received a Ph.D. in psychology from Stanford University and subsequently held positions at Educational Testing Service, Indiana University, the University of Maryland, Virginia Department of Education, Cherry Creek (Colorado) Schools, and the Alliance for Curriculum Reform. He is currently an independent researcher, policy analyst, and writer located in Alexandria, Virginia. He is the author of *Transforming America's Schools: A Prescription for Getting Past Blame*, published in 1994 by the American Association of School Administrators. He was the first Distinguished Fellow of the Agency for Instructional Technology in 1994–95 and his research in this role produced a book published by the TECHNOS Press of AIT (Bloomington, Ind.), *Final Exam: A Study of the Perpetual Scrutiny of American Education*. Bracey also has a forthcoming book from Educational Research Services tentatively titled *Statistics for People Who Hate Statistics*.

Bracey may be reached at 3333 Helen St., Alexandria, VA 22305-2627. Phone: 703-519-0735.